It's Not A Big Thing In Life

It's Not A Big Thing In Life

In Life

Strategies for Coping

Considerations for
My Adult Grandchildren

Arnie Witkin

This is dedicated to the ones I love, Roni, David and Samantha, Michael and Helena, Sarah, Sophia, Deni, Ansel, Ari and Natalya. The biggest thing in my life is my family. Everything I do, I do for you. My wish for you is that you grow up in good health, with solid values, being self-reliant and having strong self-esteem.

Contents

Acknowledgements

First and foremost I would like to thank my wife, Roni. Love is laughing at your partner's jokes over and over and over again. Also patiently listening to your theories over and over and over again and smiling each time. Roni has been my rock and my support for 47 years. When I was drained by the Covid-19 pandemic, she encouraged me to show some grit and persevere. Without that gentle prodding I could easily have given up.

I would like to thank my editors, Deborah Rudman, Vanessa Valkin and Carol Trow, who all played a vital role at different stages of the creation. I apologise for my continual toing and froing and for your patience in handling it.

I am extremely grateful to Dov Fedler, the doyen of cartoonists, for his magnificent illustrations. He's been at the top of his game for nearly 60 years and has lost none of his skill and perspicacity.

Reina Teeger, Lynnette Baskind, Connie Valkin, Balfour Valkin, Estelle Doctor, Talya Matuson, Ian Clark and Bess Teeger were my 'focus group' who read the drafts and gave me valuable feedback. It was actually their encouragement and favourable assessments that made me believe that maybe I really did have something valuable to say.

Having never been on any social media I was quite terrified of producing a website. Tess Harris and Borislav Bonchev dispelled all my fears and built something that I'm really proud of: www.arniewitkin.com.

Michael Holding gave me a copy of his autobiography, *No Holding Back*. Inside he wrote, 'To my dear friend Arnie. From one cricketer to another.' Acknowledging that he is an icon and probably the most feared fast bowler of his generation, I said, 'Mikey, you were a cricketer – I played cricket.' But his words are a microcosm of the man. Behind his great strength he is thoughtful and sensitive, although he told me that in the heat of the battle he could be quite fierce. My life has been greatly enriched by his friendship. Thank you Mikey for your lovely foreword – from one author to another!

My thanks to Caroline Towndrow and Ania Kalinowska of LifeBook for ironing out the wrinkles and preparing the book for publication and to Roy Moëd and Yvette Conn for making the facility available to me.

Lastly, thanks to Trish Hughes and Aleena Deandra of MPS Executive Suites for completing the very complex (for me) task of loading my book on to Amazon. They took away all the anxiety of a technophobe.

Foreword by Michael Holding

West Indian test cricketer
Cricket commentator and pundit for Sky Sports and SuperSport

Life! Life is what you make it. I heard that expression on so many occasions as a young man growing up. And for the most part, that expression is true, but we also have to acknowledge that there are some of us who have had no hand in the shape of our lives. Whether it was because of the country of our birth or the circumstances we were born into, life just happened and we made the best of it.

I have to say I have been very fortunate in having the opportunity to largely shape my life and part of that good fortune has been to travel the world and meet some great people and make lasting friendships. One such friendship has been with Arnie Witkin and his wife Roni. We met under the weirdest of circumstances through his son David, whom I met in South Africa during the 2003 cricket World Cup tournament, in a casino around a roulette table, no less. At the end of the night, David and a friend of his offered me a lift back to my hotel, which I gladly accepted. We had a cordial chat and on dropping me off David handed me his telephone number saying he lived in London and if I felt like catching up in the next UK summer while I was there working for SKY, I should give him a call.

I don't think that he expected me to call because I hadn't offered him my number, so when I did, he had no idea who the strange number that registered on his phone belonged to. I had to tell him twice and the second time I added 'Holding' to 'Michael' and finally it registered. That led to an invitation to his parents' home in St John's Wood, where

I met Arnie and Roni. Now, anyone who has met Arnie knows he is an accomplished orator and the cancer he refers to in these pages that has robbed him of 30% of his voice has not slowed him down. On many an occasion he has had us in fits of laughter when he makes his obligatory speeches at his 'cricket parties'. If you're fortunate enough to be handed one of his current business cards, you will see it reads, 'Speech Writer/ Public Speaking Coach/ Executive Coach and Mentor', so it should be no wonder that he has decided to put pen to paper.

I have found Arnie to be generous, kind, deep thinking, easy going and humorous – and a passionate cricket lover. He is most engaging and I have noticed that he practices what he preaches – he makes almost everybody that comes into contact with him feel good about themselves. I imagine that he must be a wonderful father and grandfather.

The title suggests that these memoirs are for his grandchildren, but they are valuable musings for any and everyone. As we go through life, those of us lucky enough to shape our own lives have to make decisions along the way. As he says, you may not necessarily agree with the reasoning behind his decisions, but it is important that you at least give them serious consideration.

As you go through the pages, you'll find a lot of humour, as life is supposed to have its frivolity and fun. I can only hope folks will enjoy the pages, as I have, and we learn to appreciate a thing or two about life from an all-rounder who has experienced his fair share of thorns and roses.

Arnie, thank you for the privilege of writing these few words as the foreword to your book. Hopefully it will be well received by many.

Introduction

My life was about to be transformed. All I had to do was to convince the board of the Legal and General Assurance Company of South Africa (L&G) to back me in a private equity venture. I would become the CEO of the company and would have significant equity. I was the extremely successful investment manager of L&G, which had been the top performing institution in South Africa for each of the previous five years. In 1982, there were no formalised private equity funds in South Africa. My proposal was well considered and comprehensive.

I had printed out my proposal and was going over it at the breakfast table. My son, David, age 6, had something of a fine motor coordination problem. He knocked over his glass of milk and some of it went onto my papers. 'Dad,' he said nervously, 'I've spilt the milk, are you cross?' I was furious, but his terrified expression melted me. 'No, Davey, I'm not cross, my darling. It's not a big thing in life. Let's clean it up and be more careful next time.' Visible relief.

A few minutes later he was fiddling with one of the pages and, being a little soggy, it tore. 'Dad, I've torn your page. Are you cross?' Now I wanted to strangle him, but once again his curly hair and cherubic face overwhelmed me. 'No, Davey, I'm not cross,' I said in a gentle voice. 'You didn't do it on purpose. Just be more careful next time.' Anxiety vaporised, broad smile. 'Dad, is it not a big thing in life?' 'No, Davey, it isn't.'

He looked lost in thought for a while, contemplating the universe. 'Dad, what is a big thing in life?'

Now I had a problem. Getting him to school and finishing my final preparation were more pressing than any cosmogony or deep philosophical discussion. So, I kicked for touch. 'I don't know, son, but that isn't.'

This book is all about the big and less big things in life and the energy that we assign to each. I often say, 'It's not a big thing in life. Very few things are.'

P.S. L&G backed my proposition and it did change the course of my life. The company was called New Bernica. Although maybe that was the course of my life!

Why This Book Now?
I recline on my balcony, gazing at the golden ocean that reflects the burning hot sun as it descends. I too am reflecting. This sunset, in all its beauty, is symbolic, metaphoric; it is the sunset of my life. I begin to contemplate the big and less big things in life. I am financially secure,

I have a beautiful and accomplished wife, two sons and two daughters-in-law, six fantastic grandchildren (I'm just a proud grandfather), who enrich my life with immense joy and pride, and a wide circle of close friends. I've led a most interesting life. I was a distinguished business person and was referred to as the 'father' of private equity in South Africa. I've been a confidant to many and have rubbed shoulders with famous business people, sports stars and celebrities.

However, the staggering reality is that, for as long as I can remember, my life has been a succession of problems, difficulties and conflicts, interspersed with successes, large and small. A never-ending obstacle course through the jungle of life. Much to my astonishment, at the ever so sprightly age of 76, it still persists. These days I am more accepting that peace of mind comes in spurts.

Pity the dusk takes us all. I have had cancer for the past 19 years. It has been quiescent for intermittent periods, but I live with the fact that it can accelerate at any time. Mortality removes us from the equation. I sigh. My life has mattered, mattered to those I love and who love me. The only way that I can think of being ever-present in their lives is to leave them, particularly my grandchildren, with the ideas and thoughts that have woven themselves into who I was, how I lived and who I became. Ideas that will hopefully liberate the mind and serve as a benchmark that addresses life's toughest hurdles.

I'd like to share my joys, struggles, failures, successes, mistakes, triumphs and coping mechanisms. The stuff of life that created the uniqueness of my fabric. Hopefully, you will peruse these pages, chuckle, frown, dismiss or embrace paragraphs or even chapters. It is particularly for my grandchildren and grandchildren worldwide that I write these words, with love and sincerity.

In this digital age, human interaction, opinion, analysis and even emotion are moulded by algorithms, social media, artificial intelligence, Google, apps and omnipresent smart phones. However, the human condition is exactly the same as it always has been. Technology has evolved but our machinery is as perfect and as flawed as at inception. People need both real and emotional intelligence to deal with their ever-changing emotions and responses to life's darts and spears, as well as to its successes. The desire for love and acceptance and for having a meaningful life is as fresh today as ever.

As a boy, I was obese and experienced great difficulty dealing with the teenage emotions that being overweight entails. Between the ages of 13 and 16, religion fascinated me. At 17, it lost its allure. My relationship with money has been similar to the weather. Periods of being caught in the rain without an umbrella to having more than enough for a rainy day. I have experienced great disappointments in my relationships with women, but then found the love of my life, when I met my wife, Roni. My marriage has been through difficult periods but has come out stronger. Thyroid cancer claimed me as a victim in 2001. The operation led to the loss of my voice for three years. Eight years later, it spread to my lungs and is still there. I have had to deal with prostate cancer, a prostatectomy and the side effects for the past 11 years. I have developed strategies for coping that have helped me to remain positive and productive.

What you will read are all my personal beliefs based on my own experience and observations; it is not necessarily all applicable to everyone. When I use words like 'Do', 'Don't', 'Always' or 'Never' they are not meant to be prescriptive – they are just for your consideration. Your own experiences will make the points more 'real'. Treat these thoughts as another source of information such as you receive all the time from social media, books, TV, friends, YouTube, parents, teachers, songs, aphorisms, TED talks, movies, etc.

If there is something that resonates with you, use it. If not, let whatever I say flow in and flow out, without taking up any emotional time. Even if you disagree with what's 'suggested' that's good – at least you will have given it consideration.

There are hundreds of books and innumerable websites on each of the topics that I cover here only briefly. Books and websites on motivation, overcoming fear, negotiating effectively, mental fortitude, resilience, relationships, sex and others can help provide greater depth and offer tools for navigating life.

There is a large amount of information. You may want to digest it in bite sizes and not all at once. You can refer to it at any time, in non-sequential order. If you experience a bump in the road or a tricky dilemma it is most likely that it will be addressed.

As it is, you will make your own decisions and process and handle, in your own way, whatever comes. Perhaps something in these musings will be part of your decision-making process; perhaps they won't. Either way, I am on your side.

Chapter 1

General Principles

Life is like a three-legged stool. One leg is love, one is money and the other is health, physical and mental. On top of the stool sit all your interests, passions, hobbies and activities. How happy will you be with all the money in the world if you have no love or your health is poor? And what's the point of being in perfect health if you have no money or love? And all the love in the world won't help if you can't afford to pay your bills or your health is bad.

However, if one leg is missing you can still have a good life and be productive in many areas. Stephen Hawking was totally disabled but still made a huge contribution to the world. I have cancer, but thankfully I am not in pain. I think that my life is blessed.

When you have all three, you are very likely to be 'happy', but to be really happy you also need to have self-esteem. Even with all those attributes, you will experience periods of desperate unhappiness if you encounter any great loss or trauma. In addition, everyday life has its challenges and uncertainties. I found that 'money' didn't necessarily mean having a big house or an expensive car. It was the preciousness of having a good job and of being able to build up sufficient capital for my advanced years.

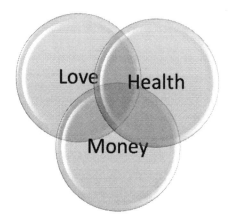

Where these three elements all cross over each other, it's Happiness

Different priorities surface at different times over the course of life. In your early adult life, love will be your dominant concern. In the middle years, money, as you establish your career, as well as children are usually the focus. As you get older, your health will become a priority.

There is a great deal about love later on, but at this stage I urge you to stop and consider this – 'The only way to get love is to be loving'. If you think that you aren't loved, you should ask yourself whether you are giving love. Are you being self-centred and demanding? Or are you being considerate and thoughtful?

A great many of my paradigms arise from when, aged just 21, I went to live in London in 1966. I didn't know anybody, it was the first time I had left South Africa and I had to survive and make a life for myself.

I had no family or friends there, so I had to develop strategies for coping on my own. I would make copious notes of what to do and what not to do, based on my interactions.

For me, these general principles apply to most situations in life:

Right and Wrong

My guiding principle is to do what I think is right and don't do what I think is wrong. These are mutually exclusive. Unfortunately, nobody is perfect and there have been many times when I did something that I wasn't proud of and didn't do something that I knew that I should have done.

As investment manager of L&G I was offered a bribe. It would have meant a lot of money for me at a time that I needed it. That was an easy decision to not do what I thought was wrong.

More difficult was when a friend of mine at school was being pushed around by some bigger boys. I knew that I should have gone to his assistance, but I slunk away, afraid that I would be the next target. I was somewhat ashamed that I didn't do what I thought was right.

An example of doing what I thought was right was at the time of the Gulf War in 2003. America was preparing to invade Iraq. George Bush had said that if Saddam Hussein would go into exile, then they would not invade. There was a 'Stop The War' rally in Hyde Park. I turned on the TV that morning and the placards read, 'Bush and Blair wanted for murder'.

Saddam Hussein, the real culprit, was one of the most vicious dictators of modern times. He had murdered or maimed close to a million people. I was strongly against the war but was incensed by the hatred towards the democratically elected leaders of the freest countries in the world. I also decided to join the rally. However, I made myself a placard that read, 'Saddam, Stop the War. Go into exile now.'

The atmosphere at the rally was electric, with over a million people. The fire and brimstone speeches stoked the anti-American and anti-Blair fervour. People were baying for their blood. I was literally one in a million who opposed the sadistic and brutal Iraqi regime, whilst at the same time being anti-war.

Four people spoke to me. A softly spoken couple from Nottingham said that mine was the only sane message. Whilst they were anti-war, they were horrified at the vitriol shown towards their own prime minister. Another was a young man, probably around 25, who asked to take a photograph with me. He said that my poster was one of the bravest things he had ever seen.

A concerned 'elderly' woman said, 'Sir, don't you think that you're taking your life in your hands with that poster?' 'Ma'am,' I said, 'This is London, not Baghdad. There is freedom here.'

The fourth was an Eastern European gentleman who said, 'Why send him into exile? Bring him here and I'll kill him myself.'

Whilst my action was something similar to jousting at windmills in what it achieved, nonetheless I did what I thought was right. Who knows, if a million people had carried my message, it may have had some effect on Saddam Hussein. Instead, he must have been basking in the thought that the British people, and others all over the world, were condoning his brutality.

I have no idea whether my poster was picked up by any of the TV broadcasts. I did walk in front of the cameras.

I admire people like Nelson Mandela and Martin Luther King who had the deep belief and courage to do what they thought was right. Liberty and life weren't as important as fulfilling what they believed was their destiny.

In the fifties, Nelson Mandela worked for my uncle in the law firm Witkin, Sidelsky and Eidelman. I met him at a function in 1999. I introduced myself saying that I was Arnie Witkin. 'Ah, Witkin,' he said, 'Are you related to Bill Witkin?' When I said I was, he asked me to contact two of the partners at the time, Laz Sidelsky and Nat Bregman, and come and have dinner with him. 'You are part of the family. I owe a lot to that firm.' He is one of the greatest examples of resilience, courage, perseverance, forgiveness and an immutable belief in his values.

When you do things that make you feel good it is likely that you are doing what you think is right.

If you would be proud to put your action on your social media page (if you have one) then it is probably right. The opposite is also true. When you do something that would embarrass you if it was on your social media page it is likely that it was 'wrong'.

On the Way to Success

My definition of success is to be the best me that I can be.

Growing up, I ate, drank and slept cricket. My parents once bought me some wicketkeeper's gloves. I fell asleep in them. If only I had a photograph of that innocent 9-year-old with his wicketkeeping gloves over the blankets. We had a tennis court, which doubled as a cricket field. If there was nobody to play with, I would bowl to makeshift wickets, usually the roller. Regrettably, my enthusiasm exceeded my ability by quite a margin.

However, the more I practised, the better I became, so that the ratio of enthusiasm to ability went from say 20 to 1 to around 3 to 1 at my best. The very top was simply out of reach, like Tantalus who couldn't quite reach the overhanging fruit or drink from the receding water. However, I was the most successful player in the second division. My enjoyment level was in direct proportion to the best me I could be. Not everyone can be number one.

Over the years I found you need the following to be successful:

Purpose and vision – you need a strong sense of where you want to get to. It's why you get out of bed in the morning. You may even have a dream.

Competence – you must be excellent at what you do.

Belief in yourself – this is not the same as arrogance; it's just a quiet belief that you can accomplish whatever you set your mind to.

Positive mental attitude – I can do this, I can get over the hurdles. I am enthusiastic about this endeavour. Not a defeatist attitude that things are too difficult.

Getting things done – successful people get things done. There is a school of thought that says 'It's more important to *do* than to *be*.' Activity is genius.

Discipline – imagine the energy and effort of elite athletes in their bid to reach the top. Hours and hours of repetitive actions. Swimmers do hundreds of lengths a day, golfers hit a thousand balls a day when practising, and the road is the office of runners. The same is required in business.

Perseverance and determination – things always go wrong and need fixing. Nearly all successful people will point to perseverance as key to their success.

Resilience and mental toughness – the strongest steel is forged in the hottest fire.

Courage – aligned with resilience. In times of crisis you may need courage to take difficult decisions and steel to follow through.

Honesty – without honesty, all the attributes in the world are practically worthless. You will be found out and face humiliation, if not prison.

Self-reliance

In 1965, at 21, I was told by a girl, with whom I was particularly infatuated, never to call her again. She said that I was a nice person but that I was immature (read: not much experience with women), tied to my mother's apron strings (read: not much experience with women) and that we weren't on the same intellectual level (read: boring accountant and brilliant English student).

Devastation would have been mild compared to what I felt. Popped balloons spring to mind.

This was one of the most defining moments in my life.

Two things could have happened. I could have succumbed to wallowing in self-pity and been afraid to ever get involved again, forever living a lonely life. Or I could have dug deep and shown some steel. As

I drove home, I had an epiphany. I determined to 'grow up'. I thought that she wouldn't have said those things if they weren't true. I went into my parents' bedroom and announced that when my accountancy apprenticeship was finished in three months I was going to London. Coming from a protected and insular background, my parents were concerned. My mother was particularly anxious, but I stood firm. I had a bit of money saved up and nothing would stop me.

In 1966, I arrived at Victoria Station in London knowing not a soul apart from my 17-year-old cousin, Elise, who lived with a family in Crystal Palace, about 45 minutes by car from Central London. I went to the Overseas Visitors Club in Earls Court and sat on my bed thinking, 'What do I do now?' I had nobody to talk to – a phone call to South Africa had to be booked with British Telecom and an appointment made for a specific time. There were no mobile phones, so any calls I made were from public phone boxes. There was no internet, no email, no WhatsApp, no Instagram. Communication was cumbersome and slow.

I had no friends or acquaintances with whom I could discuss how I felt, or to ask advice from or to just have a drink with. I did some of the usual sightseeing on my own but was too afraid to speak to almost anyone, other than perfunctorily. I had a physical constriction around my chest because I was so tense and afraid.

I did have a very close friend who was studying medicine in Edinburgh, so after a few days, I wrote to him and arranged to visit him for a couple of weeks. Fortunately, mail in the UK was delivered the next day. He shared a house with two friends and was well established. It was a relief to be able to mix with friendly people again. But eventually I had to return to London to the Overseas Visitors Club where I needed to sort my life out. There was no point in blaming my parents or my upbringing or God or my teachers or anyone else for my situation. There I was – only me. If I didn't take charge of my life, who would? I just wanted someone to come forward and sort out my life, but there was no one.

I wrote down my priorities – accommodation, work, transport, social life, sport – and made a plan for each one. I was solely responsible for myself. It was liberating to be independent and self-reliant.

I realised that responsibility is total. If you are shipwrecked on a desert island, there is no point in lying on the sand crying and moaning about your lot or blaming all and sundry. By all means be upset, but then you need to get up and try to sort out some shelter.

My father organised three job interviews for me. Out of politeness I went to all three and was offered three jobs. I declined them all because I wanted to find my own. I saw an advertisement by a recruitment agency for a chartered accountant at a 'London Club'. Being sure it was a football, golf or cricket club, I applied. I gasped when the lady said that it wasn't a sports club. 'What other kind of club is there?' I naively asked. 'The Playboy Club,' she said. I burst out laughing. 'I couldn't do that. What will my mother say?' Cheekily she said, 'Let's find out.' She called the Playboy Club and arranged an interview. It lasted two hours and they offered me the job. My mother was indeed shocked, but she accepted it! The juxtaposition of the 'immature' Johannesburg boy and one of the most sophisticated fleshpots in the world was stark. The incongruity and irony were not lost on me.

London 1966 was when I became entirely responsible for myself.

P.S. I bumped into the girl a few years later at a dinner party. She was married with three children and I was also married. At the time I had had some moderate success and was fairly well known. She recalled the fateful day at the Emmarentia delta. She said, 'I was an arrogant, stuck up, self-centred bitch. But I was correct about the intellectual level. Yours was higher.'

Expectations and Demands

I have a strong belief that you can have no expectations or make demands of anybody.

The opposite of self-responsibility is having expectations of and making demands on people. There is a difference between having a reasonable 'expectation' in the form of an anticipation that someone will act in a certain way. For instance, you may expect or anticipate that your partner will call you when they say they will. But you can't have the expectation or demand that they do. They may be busy or not want to talk to you at that moment. Taking responsibility for yourself will result in patience and understanding. By demanding the phone call, you are putting pressure on the other person for your own needs to talk at that moment.

Some examples of expectations or demands:

- ➢ I expect you to make dinner.
- ➢ I insist that you give up snooker after work.
- ➢ I expect you to buy me flowers every Friday.
- ➢ I expect you to wear only modest clothes.
- ➢ I expect you to give me a place to stay for the weekend.
- ➢ Stop whatever you're doing and collect me from my office.

The list is endless.

I believe that all of those things could be in the form of a request, which can be refused. If they are, you then need to take responsibility for making different arrangements.

I'm not sure how I would handle situations for which I was clearly not responsible. For instance, you may be a victim of a sexting bully. He or she has circulated an intimate image of you which was sent in good faith. Suddenly your naked body is all over the internet. How do you take responsibility? It is perfectly reasonable to 'expect' or even 'demand' that personal material would remain confidential. Before you send intimate images of yourself give it very serious consideration. What seems like fun and daring can end up being quite heart-breaking.

Despite your shock and embarrassment, you still need to make a decision going forward. You are responsible for that decision. It may be that you should go to the police, or ignore it, or retaliate in some way. Certainly you could discuss it with parents, friends or a lawyer. Whatever it is, it is up to you. You need to summon all your mental strength, take charge of your life and develop a strategy for coping. It is likely best that you accept responsibility for having sent the image in the first place and then look for a course of action.

If you are in some trouble, there is a very reasonable expectation that your family or friends may help you. But the circumstances may be such that, by sticking with you, they are opening themselves to criticism or even punishment. For instance, you confide in a friend that you have committed an offence and you want them to give you an alibi. If they do, they could have a problem with the authorities. They shouldn't put themselves in this position and you shouldn't expect them to.

A vivid example: your boyfriend or girlfriend smokes and you hate smoking. There is a strong difference between saying 'I expect you to give up smoking or I'm leaving' and 'I can't expect you to stop smoking, but I can't live with smoking.' The second statement gives the smoker the choice and you are in control. The first is an ultimatum and puts the smoker on the defensive.

In some situations, the expectations you may have are entirely necessary. For instance, 'I expect you not to physically or emotionally harm me.' If you are being abused, it is your responsibility to leave the relationship. There may be a financial cost which needs to be taken into consideration.

The circular problem is, 'Can I expect you to have no expectations?' My way of handling that is, 'You can have expectations if you want to, but unfortunately I can't always live up to them.'

A miraculous solution to most problems. Write everything down and make a plan!

In 1989, Roni and I emigrated to London. I did some consulting for a merchant bank. The chief executive, to whom I reported, was fired in 1991 and I had no regular work. For the next three years, I tried to replicate my South Africa formula and met with venture capitalists, merchant banks and boutique consultants. I made the acquaintance of a few brick walls. I was in a downward spiral and was unable to shake myself out of it.

On a very bad day, I locked myself in my study, cleared my desk, took a sheet of paper, and focused on writing down everything that was bothering me. I had seven issues – career, cash flow, tax query in South Africa, domestic issue with my son, lack of self-esteem and self-confidence, painful tennis elbow restricting my cricket and feeling quite depressed – and just brainstormed – what outcomes I wanted, my feelings, my anxieties, reality as opposed to blind fear, who could help me, what would happen if the status quo continued, what was in my control and what wasn't, what options I had and the consequences of each. Just everything.

There is no such thing as no decision. By definition, your action is your decision, whether you think it is or not. I realised that I had 'decided' to stay in this state of inertia, even though it was slowly destroying me. Internal conflict is when your body and your mind are not in the same place. This conflict can have many levels. At red alert, action is required. The status quo will be destructive. At lower levels, the conflict may be a state of ambivalence or mixed feelings. One of the most prevalent of human emotions is ambivalence. 'I'm not entirely happy, but there are many compensations.' I was at the highest level. I had to set about getting my body to where my mind was.

When everything was written down, my fears all became concrete, exorcising the invisible ghosts floating around my psyche. Four of the problems disappeared immediately as I saw that the reality was really quite benign – not big things in life in the light of day and easily fixable. It is like being in a hot air balloon. To get lift off, you need to jettison the sandbags that are weighing you down.

The tax query was out of my control, so why worry? In the event the revenue agreed with me.

For the lack of self-esteem and self-confidence my plan was to seek counselling. After all, I had been successful in the past. When a diamond falls into the mud it is still a diamond.

What remained was earning money and a career.

One of the possibilities was to come back to do business in South Africa, where I was well known. Before I wrote it down, in my head there were many reasons why it was a bad idea and I'd rejected it a few times. Splitting up a young family for a week a month, too much travelling, I needed a partner in SA, which I didn't have, would I be crawling back with my tail between my legs? When I wrote everything down, the solution exploded out of the page. It was patently obvious that this would solve the problem of current income and a long-term career.

Visualisation was also important. I could see myself as the executive chairman of a listed company successfully doing what I did before. And then I had to act on the plan, which I did. I went back to do business in South Africa. The institutions that had backed me in New Bernica were only too willing to do so again. I was once again successful.

You can use the GROW model, which is used by coaches and mentors. It's on the internet. I speak to a lot of people in very senior positions who confide in me and when I ask them if they've written down the problem, very few, if any, have.

G. What is your **Goal**? What outcome do you want? Visualise in detail what you want to achieve

R. What is the **Reality**? What are the facts on the ground? Write down everything you can think of relating to your problem.

O. What **Options** do I have? Write down all the possibilities and the consequences of each option

W. What is my **Will** – my intention? What is my plan? What will I do?

Other factors:

Who can help me? This is crucial

What is in my control? How can I leverage it?

What is in the control of someone else? How can I influence them?

What is in control of the environment? What steps can I take to adjust to the environment?

If you are unable to move your body to where your mind is, or vice versa, you will remain in conflict. People stay in poor relationships or dead end jobs, in a state of ambivalence, for years and even decades. If you are in a relationship or job that isn't perfect, you may as well try to make it as pleasant as possible. What's the point of bickering or whinging?

I heard an interview recently with Clive Woodward. He was the head coach of the England rugby team that won the World Cup in 2003 and he was Director of Elite Performance of the British Olympic Association. He currently runs a leadership consultancy company. He was asked what the best advice he had ever had was, and he replied, 'Writing things down.'

Without a plan, you just have anxiety. When you have a plan, you can act to your greatest advantage.

With a plan you go from anxiety to action.

Unfortunately not all plans come together. However you have a much greater chance of success by making a conscious plan than by having a de facto plan, which would be the status quo.

The most powerful force in the world is focus. Laser beams are focused energy. You need to make a conscious choice about where to focus your energy.

To illustrate the importance of clearing your head I asked two of my mentees from Ort Jet in Cape Town to tell of their experiences with writing things down.

This from Doryce Sher:
At my first mentoring session Arnie listened with intense concentration for 45 minutes and then quietly and gently said,

'You've done well; you are 75% of the way there.'

I was emotionally in a deep black hole and felt about 5% 'of the way there'. His words put a spring in my step for the first time in many months. Every session with Arnie was one of him listening and then relating a relevant story and pearls of wisdom – a moral from each story relevant to my obstacle. After every session I was stimulated and energised. I felt that he really cared. I went home with my 'homework' of writing things down and being accountable to him.

Arnie's attributes of excellent listener, patience, consistent reliability, encouragement, belief in me, and his quiet and powerful observations took me from the 5% faith to 100%. The rest was my writing everything down, making plans and implementing them. Without a doubt this was the key.

From Jason Sandler:
Arnie is a most wonderful listener and is always open to give his thoughts and opinions. He has a knack to direct you where you should be going in a manner that it feels as if the answers are coming from within yourself. The greatest advice he ever gave me was to take my problems and write them down and just keep writing until the plan just emerges. Boy does this work!

One of the greatest inhibitors of creativity is clutter. How do you find diamonds if you're mired in rubble? Focus requires nothing in the way. Say you're working on your computer and out of the corner of your eye you spot an article you've cut out of a magazine. You pick it up and the distraction has ruined your concentration and watered down your train of thought.

In business it is particularly important to have a neat and tidy desk. I was friendly with the chief executive of one of the biggest companies in South Africa. He had a very large office with a desk more than half the size of a table tennis table. When you had a meeting with him the desk was empty. I once walked into his office without notice. He had one file open and he was working on one paper to do with the subject. On the far right-hand side of the desk were three or four files, neatly placed and overlapping, for all his open matters. He was the clearest thinker I have ever met.

A Sense of Humour

> *'Humour is mankind's greatest pleasure.'*
>
> Mark Twain

I cannot stress too strongly how important it is to develop a sense of humour. It's so important as to almost be a fourth leg to the Money, Health and Love paradigm. If it doesn't come naturally to you to tell jokes or make puns, then at least you can appreciate others' humour. In their book, *Humour Seriously* (Penguin, 2020), the authors Jennifer Aaker and Naomi Bagdonis talk about the generosity of laughter. Laughing at people's jokes makes them feel good about themselves.

Most advertisements for partners on dating apps or in newspapers will say that the person is looking for someone with a good sense of humour (GSOH). I was very lucky that I loved words and had an acute sense of humour, particularly when I or others made witty, off the cuff remarks. I was quite good at telling jokes but if they had a particularly funny and unexpected ending, I sometimes couldn't finish the joke because I was laughing so much. One such joke is:

I have an inexplicable phobia about intricately designed groups of buildings. It's called a complex complex complex.

It happened once when I was making an investment presentation to a group of prospective clients for L&G and there I was bent over the lectern in fits of laughter. Fortunately, it looked so ridiculous that the audience started laughing with me. We got the business.

Think of people you enjoy being with. Chances are that the people you enjoy most are those who make you laugh and who you make laugh. Laughter creates intimacy.

The monthly magazine *Reader's Digest* used to run a series of jokes, the heading of which was 'Laughter, the Best Medicine'.

I was quite shy but adept at clever puns and witty repartee. This would attract the attention of the more astute girls (and guys). My friends and I who had a similar sense of humour would spend whole evenings laughing. Girls who didn't appreciate my sense of humour didn't hang around too long …

I was particularly aware of any hidden sensitivities of the people I was talking to. 'Ribbing' someone is fine when you know them extremely well, but even then you need to be careful. Always laugh *with* people, not at people. Friendly banter can cement friendships, because you know each other's limits. However a really nasty remark can damage a relationship for ever.

If you see that someone has even the slightest discomfort, stop immediately. You never know what anyone is going through. Be aware of your own feelings when you make these 'friendly digs'. Underneath it all, I wonder if there's really such a thing as a friendly 'dig'. There may be something more to it than just being funny. For instance, I can remember saying something about a friend that was funny on the surface but not very nice. When I thought about my motives, I realised that I was really trying to bring him down a notch and elevate myself in front of the group. I was disappointed in myself, because the remark was quite nasty and, in fact, not very funny at all. I'm now very careful and almost never taunt anybody, even among my closest friends. Certainly, I would never 'diss' anybody. It is senseless and hurtful.

Marriage is a rich source of jokes – usually along the lines of how difficult it is. For instance, 'Every time I argue with my husband, words flail me.' 'I had words with my wife last night, but I never got a chance to say mine.' These can be very funny and can be laughed at by both partners, except when the so-called joke is malicious or humiliating. We had a friend once who thought he was being funny when he said in a joking tone that when he married his wife it ruined his chances of finding anyone else. The problem was that their marriage was quite rocky at the time and it was clear she was uncomfortable. We stopped being friends with them. Jokes about relationships are delicate and can only be told when it is clear that the joke is actually the opposite of what it purports to be.

One temperature gauge regarding the health of a relationship is how much genuine laughter there is.

The most important aspect of a sense of humour is to be able to laugh at yourself. Self-deprecating jokes are usually well received and are quite endearing. If someone says something nasty about you, the best defence is to make a joke about it and laugh at yourself.

My son David began his high school education in London as a 13-year-old at the City of London School, established in 1452. On his first day, some of the boys teased him by singing a satirical song, 'I've never met a nice South African'. He came home and told me that he was feeling hurt about this and that they also teased him about his height. I suggested to him that when they sing the song he should not take it personally (bullies are actually insecure). He should multiply by three and laugh. That way it would be like them hammering a nail into jam – no resistance.

When challenged at school the next day he said, 'Nice South Africans went out with the dodo and you should see me when I stand up.' And he laughed. The bullies were flummoxed. I also showed him a photograph of the South African rugby team in the mid-1960s and pointed out that the captain was Dawie de Villiers, who was five foot five (168cm) in a team where nearly everyone was over six feet (183cm). On his fourteenth birthday, three months after the incident, 12 boys arrived at our front door with a huge cake. They came to give him a surprise party. In time, David became head boy of the school.

One of the quickest ways to establish rapport in any surrounding is to make a witty remark that is truly funny and appreciated. Before every business meeting I would infer something humorous. It nearly always broke the ice. Humour works particularly well in a work or business setting. However, the joke has to be appropriate. When I had a confrontational meeting ending a partnership there was no place for humour. I had to show that I was deadly serious.

I believe that you will never laugh at the joke of someone you don't like. As a rather insecure teenager, there were guys I didn't like and if they were telling a joke I would either walk away or, if I couldn't, I would try not to laugh, however funny it may have been. I didn't want to give them the satisfaction of seeing me laugh. It actually said more about me than the joke teller. But if someone doesn't laugh at your joke, it doesn't necessarily mean they don't like you. It could be that it wasn't so funny!

Surround yourself with people who make you laugh and who you make laugh. I laugh all the time with my friends and it is often a foundation of the relationship. I don't think that I could ever have a relationship with anyone unless there was a great deal of laughter. I'm lucky that Roni appreciates my sense of humour and we laugh a lot.

Never tell a racist or gender demeaning joke. It may sound funny to some, but people have lost their jobs and reputation for making one unguarded, throwaway line. Dean Jones, a respected Australian cricketer and commentator, once made what he thought was a harmless quip about Hashim Amla, the Muslim South African opening batsman who has a long beard. He said something about Amla looking a bit like a terrorist terrorising the Australian bowlers. He wasn't on air at the time, but it was overheard by the crew. He really had no ill intent but that was the end of his career as a commentator. An American golf commentator made an ill-conceived remark about a woman player who had large breasts. He wondered if they got in the way of her swing. He was summarily dismissed.

Rory Bremner, a renowned satirist and impersonator, said in a recent interview, 'I am one joke or comment away from ending my career.'

Independence, Dependence and Interdependence

Independence

If we compare our lives to a tree, the deepest root is the one that stabilises your growth and allows you to be independent. Your values are your roots.

With that as our foundation, we can build relationships that are based on mutual respect and admiration. We need to be independent first, before we can become interdependent (see below). Steven Covey's *The Seven Habits of Highly Successful People* (reissued by Simon and Schuster, 2020) emphasised this point.

When I left South Africa for the UK in 1966, I became independent. Cutting the umbilical cord gave me self-esteem. I started doing what I thought was right and not doing what I thought was wrong. I was away from the control of my parents and was reliant on myself for getting a job and earning my own living.

Dependence

Dependence is a reliance on others. When someone is overly dependent, they constantly ask for help for even the most basic of tasks. This level of dependence involves relying on someone else to do things for you that you should be able to do for yourself; and is usually found in people with low self-esteem. Dependence is an able-bodied person asking for help in crossing the road.

When we are very young, we are totally dependent on others. But from an early age, young children start to say, 'I can do that by myself!' As you get older, you should become less dependent on others. It is fine to occasionally ask for assistance, but that is not the same as a deep dependency.

Unhealthily dependent people can be a drain on energy and difficult to be with. They continually need reassurance, make undue demands and become possessive. They are easily offended and have little resilience, even to small setbacks. If you find that you are overly dependent, you need to work on yourself. Read articles and literature on self-assurance, assertiveness and self-esteem. Make a determined effort to become independent. You may need help to stop yourself from being needy.

Interdependence

When you're in a personal relationship, you are interdependent on each other which is a positive situation. But it can only come after you have established yourself as independent. Interdependence is where you both need each other to perform two independent functions. For instance, in a motor car there is the brake and the accelerator. While they work independently, the one can't do without the other. Members of sports teams are all independent players, but they are interdependent on their teammates for optimum performance.

The management of a hotel is dependent on housekeeping, restaurant staff, front of house staff, and reservation personnel. If one fails, all will fail. Conversely, if everyone flourishes the enterprise will succeed. We clearly need to rely on any number of people to do what they say will do

– in business and in our personal lives. Think of doctors or dentists or plumbers or electricians or hairdressers.

In *The Prophet*, Kahlil Gibran said:

'And stand together, yet not too near together: For the pillars of the temple stand apart; And the oak tree and the cypress grow not in each other's shadow.'

It is the same in relationships. Each partner will have their respective 'duties' and each should be competent in their own right. One partner may be the breadwinner and the other the homemaker. Or both might contribute to the family budget and share the household chores. The ideal is when both parties contribute confidently.

What you don't want is for one partner to be needy and keep asking for help and reassurance for routine tasks. This will lead to resentment.

I am a very independent person, but I can't imagine what it would be like without Roni or without my family or friends. At the same time I am not afraid to ask for help. In the 1990s and early 2000s I went for psychoanalysis for many years. I recently experienced a trauma with regard to the stock market collapse and the coronavirus. I temporarily went back to my therapist. This didn't detract from my ability to remain a reliable husband, father, grandfather and friend. After a few weeks, I was back to my normal, rational self. With help, I overcame my difficulties.

Overcoming Disappointments

Life is about overcoming disappointments and obstacles and then celebrating the victory, until the next disappointment, and so on. Every great businessperson – Bill Gates, Jeff Bezos, Richard Branson – will have overcome massive setbacks on their journeys. Every sports star – tennis champs Serena Williams, Roger Federer and Rafael Nadal, Formula One driver Niki Lauda, skiing champion Lindsey Vonn – overcame potentially career-changing injuries and continued to flourish.

> *Frequently, people say that their greatest growth spell has come after a distressing disappointment or failure.*

It is important to develop mental fortitude and resilience. If you are resilient, you can accept your disappointments and overcome them. However bad things seem, they will get better in time and most setbacks can be overcome. Think of the thousands of Holocaust survivors who suffered inconceivable hardship and deprivation and survived to make new, productive lives for themselves.

Mental fortitude is the ability to resist, manage and overcome doubts, concerns and circumstances that prevent you from succeeding, or excelling at a task or moving towards an objective that you set out to achieve. Taking firm decisions, based on weighing up options you have noted down, will help you to take control. If you find yourself feeling out of control, books or articles on self-reliance and taking control of your life, such as *Awaken the Giant Within* by Anthony Robbins (Free Press, 1991) may be helpful.

Resilience is achieved by acknowledging what has happened, taking responsibility, living in the moment, getting up off the floor and trying again. As Nelson Mandela said:

> *'Don't judge me by my successes. Judge me by how many times I fell and got back up again.'*

I encourage you to be kinder to yourself in your moments of despair or disappointment, regardless of how small or large they might be. At one level, be thankful for the disappointment (as long as it is not too crushing), because it gives you the opportunity for growth, learning and understanding. I recently received a letter from Lea Froman, a friend with pancreatic cancer, who gave me permission to quote it. Sadly she passed away a few weeks ago, but was extremely brave to the very end.

> 'I/we are on a fascinating journey …
> I love journeys and processes as you know I believe we never get anything to deal with we can't handle. I believe what unfolds every single day is in my highest interest.
> I'm getting so much closer to my soul and essence. I can only see this as a healing journey for me and all those around in me.
> I don't think of myself as a cancer patient much.
> I prefer to say teacher, rather than tumour …
> I feel like I've been given a gift, as a simple switch turned on the moment I heard I had a tumour on my pancreas, to only be in the now, in the present moment.

Reading, having the awareness and trying to implement Tolle's book *The Power of Now* was "work". Now it's my new way of being. I've been gifted a new mind and a new body is sure to follow.'

Clearly this is at the very highest level of resilience from an exceptionally courageous person and very few people would perceive their illness in this way. However, it is worth striving for.

Allow yourself to be disappointed about the 'smaller' things but then move on. It's not a big thing in life. Very few things are. In the words of Hans Reichenbach:

'If error is corrected whenever it is recognized as such, the path of error is the path of truth.'

'Fothers'

When David was 12 in his last year at primary school in Johannesburg, there was an organisation called the 'Johannesburg Mini Council'. It was modelled on the real City Council, but its main function was charitable. They appointed a 'mini mayor' and 'mini councillors' and had meetings to discuss how to run the council. Each school appointed two pupils to go to the council, usually the head boy and head girl.

David was almost certain that he would be appointed mini mayor at the function where all the councillors would be announced. There were 12 councillors, a mini mayor and a deputy mini mayor. David was ready with his brilliant acceptance speech.

Each councillor's name was called, then that of the deputy mini mayor, and as they were about to announce the mini mayor, David took his speech out of his pocket and got ready to go up to the podium. Horror of horrors, his name wasn't called out. Not only was he not the mini mayor, he wasn't even chosen as a councillor.

With tears welling up he said wanted to go home. I lay in bed with him and he was inconsolable. He said that he was embarrassed and couldn't face his friends. I acknowledged his feelings and I told him to stay disappointed for as long as he needed, because he had suffered a major setback. What I *didn't* do was tell him to snap out of it or that everything would be fine.

I also told him the story of Henry Fotheringham. 'Fothers' was a famous South African opening batsman. He went through a bad spell and was dropped from the Transvaal A cricket team to the Transvaal B team. This was humiliating for the South African opening batsman. I told David that Fothers had to go in to bat for Transvaal B, no matter his distraught feelings. When he faced the first ball, had he still been thinking about his disappointment, it would have hit him between the eyes. Fothers instead made 187 not out for the B team and was back in the Transvaal A team the next week.

I told David that at some point in the future – I didn't know how long, maybe a day, maybe a week, a month or a year – the disappointment would fade. In the meantime he should stay disappointed.

After about an hour David snapped his fingers and exclaimed, 'Fothers!' 'Dad,' he said, 'Tomorrow's school and I have to get on with it.'

He was lucky – it took him only a couple of hours to get over his disappointment – unlike Miss Havisham. Miss Havisham was one of the main characters in the Charles Dickens novel *Great Expectations*. She was jilted by her fiancé hours before she was due to walk down the aisle. She stopped all the clocks at the exact time she heard the news, stayed in her wedding dress and kept the table laid as it had been in readiness for the wedding celebration for 30 years. You could say that after 30 years she should get a life. What about 20 years? That's a very long time. Ten years, she would only have been 30 years old. Five years – what a waste. One year? Still a long time. A week, a day, an hour, a minute? Somewhere along that timeline you need to get your life back together. The sooner the better.

About 15 years ago, I was involved in a complex transaction. The other party was particularly devious, bordering on the illegal. I lost around £30,000, which was a lot of money for me at the time. I was stewing about it and after a few days David said to me, 'Dad, what about Fothers?' I said, 'I know, Davey, but how?' Fortunately I did apply my Fothers paradigm and after a few days I was back on track.

It's all about acknowledging your feelings, which are real, accepting them and then negotiating with them so that you can get on with life effectively. If you can't negotiate with your feelings, you may stay disappointed for a very long time.

An example of negotiating with your feelings is as follows:

About eight years ago I lost a lot of money in a poorly considered transaction. I accepted the fact that I was extremely upset. I said to myself, 'Will I hang on to this disappointment for 30 years, like Miss Havisham?' 'No.' 'Twenty years?' 'No.' 'Ten years?' 'No.' 'Five years?' 'No.' 'One year?' 'No.' 'Six months?' 'No.' 'Three months?' 'No.' 'One month?' 'I can't climb under my bed for that long.' 'A week?' 'Maybe, but I still have things to do and have to get on with life.' 'A day?' 'I'm sure I'll be upset all day, but then that's it. Tomorrow I have to make new plans.'

It took me two days to largely get over it. I say largely because it still rankled for quite a while, but the rankling diminished with each day as I made new plans. Even today there are flashes of annoyance with myself, but they are few and far between and don't last too long.

I wasn't so lucky when the coronavirus struck. Apart from the shock of the collapse of the stock market I had an existential crisis. I was on my chemotherapy drug and had I contracted the virus I would almost certainly not have survived. The combination of losing the money and the fear of dying resulted in a state close to a nervous breakdown. In addition we had to be in isolation, cut off from family and friends. I tried every one of my strategies for coping, but the feeling was also physical. No amount of negotiation helped. To overcome the tremors I took sedatives, which calmed me down. It took me about six weeks of intense work on myself before I was able to go off the medication, negotiate with my feelings and function normally again.

I met the revered Indian philosopher Swami Parthasarathy a while ago. He was a great cricket fan, something which he and I had in common. I took him to Lords Cricket ground to watch England play the West Indies. My friend was Alvin Kallicharran, a former captain of the West Indies. I asked the Swami if he would like to meet him and he said that he would love to, because he had seen him make a double century in India.

We agreed to meet behind the pavilion at teatime but 'Kalli' didn't arrive. When the Swami went to the toilet I asked the Swami's helper whether she thought that the Swami would be disappointed. 'No,' she said, 'the Swami wouldn't be disappointed about such a small thing.' When he came back I asked him if he was disappointed. 'Yes,' he answered, 'I am disappointed, but it won't affect me.' He recognised his feelings but they didn't last long. I have adopted this policy to try not to be affected, but sometimes it takes me a bit longer than it does the Swami!

When I have had disappointments in my life, I have tried to move on by getting involved in activities that interested me. I have thrown myself into work and into my hobbies such as cricket, golf and reading to take my mind off the disappointment. When I started my first company, we entered into a deal to buy into a motor dealership. It was announced in the newspapers and, for us, it was important. After a disagreement with the other party, we withdrew from the deal with some quite negative comment. My confidence was shattered, but I was aware that I had a company to run. I called all my merchant bank contacts, stockbrokers, lawyers, accountants and other intermediaries and immersed myself in finding new deals with great intensity. It worked.

Famous US author Nora Ephron was devastated when her husband left her. But her mantra became, 'Get over it.' She promptly wrote a novel (which became a movie) that paid for her next house. This strategy is excellent for moving on, if you can do it. Eventually it is most likely that you *will* 'get over it'.

Be aware that you will experience loss at every stage of life – loss of face, loss of material possessions, loss of money, loss of a loved one, loss of a lover, loss of energy, loss of youth, loss of ability, loss of good health. In every case you should formulate a strategy for coping.

Fabled singer Leonard Cohen lost all his money at age 70 to a swindle by his accountant. At his fairly advanced age he had to start touring again to make a living.

Visualisations can be very helpful in getting through difficult situations. When I had my radiotherapy for my thyroid cancer every morning and evening, I used to listen to inspirational tapes by Louise Hay. They are affirmations and meditations and I would lose myself in the idyllic imagery. It took my mind to a land of warm sunshine, lakes, waterfalls, rainbows, lush vegetation, and fields of flowers – far away from the pain. My favourite book of hers is *You Can Heal Your Life* (1984).

A book called *Consciously Creating Circumstances* (a book from 1953 by George Winslow Plummer, reissued in 2018 by the White Press) actually changed the course of my life for the better. In 1985, New Bernica was struggling. We had done two deals and I had been unable to find suitable companies. One lunchtime I walked out of my office and bumped into the girlfriend of a friend of mine. 'You don't look too happy,' she said.

I normally would not have wanted to show weakness but on this occasion I said that I was concerned that the business was not succeeding. 'Come and have some lunch with me,' she said.

We went to a nearby restaurant and she told me about Plummer's book. It wasn't the book itself that was so powerful. It was the concept that one could 'consciously create circumstances' that I found so appealing. Instead of letting things happen to me, I could go out and make things happen. I started using creative visualisations and exercising my imagination. Instead of renewing certain deposits for 12 months, I put the money we had on call so that it could be accessed immediately. Shortly thereafter we took a stake in an IT company that was the most successful deal that I have ever done. I am fairly sceptical about claims that are made by *The Secret*, a book by Rhonda Byrne (Atria Books/ Beyond Words, 2006), but positive visualisations can bring things to life. Athletes imagine the way they are going to run the race and see themselves breaking the tape. Golfers visualise exactly where they want to hit the ball. For putting they see the ball going into the hole. It's called Mental Rehearsal.

Ultimately getting over setbacks has to do with taking responsibility for yourself, even if you take responsibility for seeking professional help.

The parable of Miss Havisham is a central theme in my life. You have met her already and you will come across her again. She is central to the idea of what constitutes a big thing in life. I think that I can now answer David's question, 'What is a big thing in life?'

A big thing in life is what you think is a big thing in life at a given point and for as long as you think it is.

The really big things in my life are permanent: family, health, love, money, self-respect, independence and values such as kindness and making people feel good about themselves. You can make your own list.

Certainly, being left at the altar is potentially a far more serious event than not being chosen as mini mayor, but for David it was a big thing in life. We can't tell anyone how much their pain is worth. The beauty queen with a birthmark on her bum, that nobody can see, can still feel that she is ugly – irrational as it may seem.

Big things in life are time sensitive. Figuratively, you lose this week and the world is caving in. However there is always a game next week. My friends and I used to say, 'What difference will it make in twenty-five years' time?' In twenty-five years it won't make a difference, but right now it's hurting.

Putting Things Into Perspective

When I was 13, I was in the final of the under-18 Transvaal (now Gauteng) table tennis championships. It was best of three games. I won the first game and was leading 20-17 in the second (a game was 21 points). I lost that game. I was leading 20-17 in the third game and lost that too. I felt humiliated and wanted to crawl away and never show my face again. I hated myself for losing. I like to recount how I went to my father's office after the game. He had a client there and I told my father that I was so upset I could have shot myself. Much to my shock the client took out a gun and said, 'Here.'

It might seem like a very small thing now, but at the time it was important to me. You may be embarrassed about something, but you will find that most people don't really care what you've done. They're too busy worrying about themselves and their mistakes. I always say that when you talk about your golf game, either to your playing partners or your wife or anybody in any situation, you are talking to yourself.

Whilst it's fine to feel disappointed, it may help to get over 'smaller' things sooner when seen in juxtaposition with life-changing events. Today's minor (and often major) error or difficulty or disappointment or embarrassment or faux pas is tomorrow's anecdote, which you can laugh at. 'Do you remember the time we accidently walked out of the restaurant without paying? The owner ran after us screaming. We thought that he was going to call the police.'

My recommendation is:

'Don't get your knickers in a knot over the small things in life.'

Regrets. The Purgatory of Should've, Could've, Would've

What is the most powerful blunt instrument that we use to beat ourselves up? It's the curse of should've, could've, would've. When married to their cousin, 'if only', nearly all regrets can be summarised in those five words.

My equity dealer at L&G came into my office one day after quite a sharp rise in the stock market the previous day. 'I should have bought stocks yesterday,' he said. I took a sheet of paper and wrote on it, 'This is a formal warning. If you ever use the words "should have" again you're fired.' I said, 'All I want to know is what you are going to do now?'

The fact is – there is only the moment. No past or future, only now. What's your plan?

There are two types of regrets – those where you did something you regret and those where you *didn't* do something and you're sorry that you didn't.

'Regret for the things we did can be tempered by time; it is regret for the things we did not do that is inconsolable.'

Sydney J. Harris

The propensity for something being subject to regret is very often at a critical time in your life. Should I break up or stay in this relationship? Should I accept this job? Should I emigrate? Should I invest in this proposal? Should I punish my child? Should I speak out? Should I sell my house? Should I trust this potentially dodgy person who is very attractive? Should I give up studying to start a business?

One such critical moment is when there is a temptation in front of you. You may be offered drugs or there is the possibility of a sexual liaison that may be dangerous or even illicit. There may be something risky, but potentially exciting. These are the times that you need to be most vigilant and give serious consideration before rushing in and regretting it later.

I have had a number of regrets but I am extremely fortunate that I was able to forgive myself and move on. Most of them relate to shares I should have bought or to shares I have bought. I still have memories of them, but they take up very little energy.

Roni and I had acquaintances whom we used to see occasionally. The husband frequently was rude to his wife and I decided that I didn't want to be friends with them. I didn't invite them to my 60th birthday soiree. It was a grand affair with 120 people. The singing was done by my friends and family. It was spoken about for years in our circle. The wife, whom we both liked, phoned Roni in tears after the party. I never realised the hurt that it would cause her. We all want to belong and be included and they had been publicly excluded. I felt remorse, even though I had been true to my feelings.

One of my biggest regrets was not walking away from a business deal I did in 1997. The other party was a very charismatic entrepreneur and he ran rings around me. On at least three occasions, I knew that I should end all negotiations but felt that I was morally committed because I had verbally agreed to most of the terms. I didn't listen to my inner voice and walk away. When I realised what a mistake I had made, I felt distraught that I had acted so unprofessionally.

As it happened, the deal turned out quite well, but only because the entrepreneur managed to hoodwink other investors and we sold our shares at a reasonable profit. In the end the company collapsed completely.

Quite a serious regret was when I was on the board of a large public company and management wanted to make an investment, which I thought was a bad idea. They presented the deal at a board meeting and asked the independent directors to comment. There were some very prominent business people on the board and each one agreed to the investment. Unfortunately, I was the last to speak and I felt intimidated and didn't speak up against the deal. I think that had I been asked to speak first I probably would have expressed my doubts. It wasn't a good deal and I was seen to be part of it.

Fortunately I have no regrets about the major decisions in my life – marriage, my career, moving to the UK in 1989 and buying an apartment in Cape Town in 2002.

Generally, it's better to stick your neck out and risk failure than not to try at all. Think tortoise. 'A ship is safe in a harbour, but that's not what ships are designed for.' Albert Einstein. To avoid regret about not doing what you wanted, take active steps to do what you think is right. It may take courage to do or say something that may not be popular with the group. It also may be prudent to keep silent when you know that saying something at that moment may create antagonism or even danger. If you feel very strongly about something it may be necessary to face the antagonism. Each case is a judgement call. Sometimes you need to ask the question, 'Will I regret not doing that?'

If it's a fundamental issue relating to core values and ethics, you need to speak out, whatever the consequences. For instance, if someone or a group is behaving in a racist or malicious way to a person or group, not speaking up or not disassociating with the group can be seen as being complicit and endorsing their views or behaviour. Distance yourself as soon as possible.

Before you speak out, you should have reasonable certainty of your facts and be able to back up your opinions, especially if someone else speaks in a loud voice.

Naturally sometimes you have to be expedient, to accommodate or compromise. Provided the compromise is helpful to you and you recognise that that's what you're doing, it's a workable choice. As Christopher Morley said:

'Lots of times you have to pretend to join a parade in which you're not really interested in order to get where you're going.'

Nobody's perfect! Either way, you have to take a decision and only time will tell if you have made the correct one.

- ➢ We all do things that we're not proud of and regret. You can't change the past – 'The moving finger writes and having writ moves on. Nor all thy piety and wit shall lure it back to cancel half a line, nor all thy tears wash out a word of it,' said Persian mathematician and philosopher, Omar Khayyam.
- ➢ You need to develop a strategy to cope with regret. Write it down.
- ➢ Recognise that it has happened and watch your feelings. You probably have a choice whether to let go of the regret or hold onto it endlessly (Miss Havisham).
- ➢ Some regrets may stay with you forever, but hopefully they become just a speck over time and you can acknowledge the regret without it affecting your life.
- ➢ It can help not to bring up the subject in the future, especially if you have apologised where appropriate.
- ➢ Try not to beat yourself up, but if you find yourself in the should've, could've, would've maelstrom say to yourself, 'STOP, I don't have to go there.' Move your mind elsewhere. This was particularly helpful to me when I was berating myself about certain investments I had made which had gone wrong. My friend gave me a visualisation of keeping myself in the dog kennel. He said that I should visualise that the dog kennel was damp, dark, cold and full of rancid meat that stank. I needed to see myself escaping from the stench and into the nourishing sunshine into the beautiful garden.

Only I could emancipate myself. It took a few days, but it worked. I made decisions about the investments and the regret dissipated. I also focused on my successes

- As you will have seen a few times – most things are seven-day wonders. There are very few really big things in life
- Most people don't really care about what you've done unless they are directly affected.
- Be willing to apologise or to make recompense.
- Accept that you are only human (this is not a good excuse for the behaviour, but it's true).

Take Risks

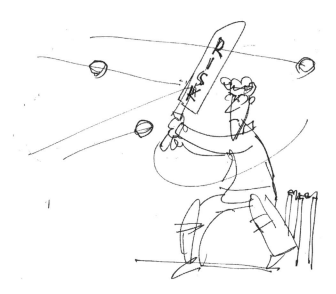

In my last year of junior school, I was chosen for the school cricket team. With my tail up and chest out I proudly told my father. 'Congratulations son,' he said. 'Great news. But be careful of the fast bowlers. Don't mess with the big boys.' Up to that time, I had never considered the possibility of being injured by a fast bowler. We were kids and although there were bowlers that were faster than others, if I got hit it wasn't too bad. It was part of the game.

My father meant no harm and was oblivious to the psychological damage that his apparently innocuous statements had on me. They stuck with me for years and there is no doubt that they hampered my development. The reality was that he had been hit on the head by a fast bowler when he was younger. He was only expressing his fear.

The result was that for a long time I was scared to take risks.

Only when I decided to go to London did I realise that the greatest risk of all is not taking a risk. You get stuck in the quicksand that is the status quo and never realise your potential.

My boss at the Playboy Club was Bill Gerhauser. Bill had been a Marine and he was scared of nothing. He could see that I was quite shy and introverted. One day he said to me, 'Arnie, what you need is exposure. Put yourself in any situation that you may have found daunting, even if means forcing yourself to do it. Don't put yourself into an obviously dangerous situation but be adventurous.' He was partly talking about taking risks with women.

He also said, 'If you are in a situation that doesn't feel right, don't panic, just let the situation flow in and flow out. Don't give it any energy. For situations that feel good, take in the sensation and enjoy it.' He warned against ever taking drugs. He said that if people around me were taking drugs, I should just observe, without judgement, and let the situation flow in and then out, but never to participate.

The result was dramatic. I decided to take more risks, particularly with women. Sometimes they came off and sometimes they didn't. When I had a poor experience, I didn't beat myself up, because at least I'd tried.

One such experience was when I wanted to play cricket in the UK. I knew of Ealing Cricket Club from a couple of colleagues from my club in Johannesburg. I was fearful of going 'cold' to a totally unknown club in a foreign country. I took Bill's advice and 'exposed' myself by going to Ealing one Sunday afternoon and announcing to the secretary that I wanted to play cricket. I was scared but as I was batting in the nets,

I thought to myself, 'I've got as much right to be here as everyone else.' I played in the First XI and continued to play for Ealing for 38 years.

Publishing this book is a great risk for me because I leave myself very exposed. However, not to publish it could lead to a regret of something undone. So I'll thank Bill Gerhauser and I hope that you do too.

Overcoming Fear

We all have fears. Some are rational and some irrational. It's in our nature to fear the worst, because if we do, our survival instinct can cause us to act to avoid the feared consequence. I have had many fears in my life, particularly the fear of not earning enough money to support my family. After my father went bankrupt, I was haunted by the image of him reduced to living in a tiny apartment in a dangerous part of town. The result is that I try to be as conservative as possible with my investments. Any fleeting fears that I have at this stage in my life I know to be unrealistic, so they disappear quite quickly.

In 1993, when I was trying to rebuild my career, I wanted to do a deal with Bear Stearns, one of the major investment banks in America at the time. I wanted them to run a 'South Africa' fund and I wanted to make the investments with them as my partners. My friend, who knew my track record and thought highly of me, was friendly with the chief executive. He introduced me to the right people. I sent them my proposition and I heard nothing for five weeks. I said to my therapist that they hadn't replied. She asked me why I hadn't followed through. I said that they were this huge company, I was just a lowly individual and that they had probably forgotten about me. I was afraid of the rejection I would get if I called them. At that moment I snapped my fingers. Another epiphany (I've had a few). I said, 'What have I got to lose?'

I called my friend and told him I hadn't heard from Bear Stearns. He immediately called the chief executive. Five minutes later I received a phone call from the person to whom I had sent my original proposal. He apologised for not getting back to me sooner. He said that they had considered my proposal but that they had decided that they needed a larger institution with whom to partner. However, he then asked me if I would become the chairman of the company. This wasn't exactly what I wanted, but it was the start of a new career for me. Apart from anything else, it really boosted my self-esteem. I was wanted by one of the biggest investment banks in the world and their partner, one of the most respected investment houses in South Africa.

By calling them and being rejected I could have lost face. But compared to what I could have gained, it was really nothing. Two of my most valuable mantras are:

What have I got to lose?
What's the worst thing that can happen if I take this action?

Of course, some fears are far more serious than anxiety about meeting new people or how to approach someone you fancy. For instance, when I received my thyroid cancer diagnosis in 2001, I was terrified. I resorted to my 'go to' strategy of writing everything down, and those fears miraculously disappeared when I could see the reality and the acceptance of 'what will be will be'. When I had my prostate cancer diagnosis in 2009 the fears were much greater because of the potential side effects of having a prostatectomy. I wrote down my strategy for coping so I was ready for them, if they happened. They weren't within my control, so one of my strategies was, once again, acceptance. More later.

How did I deal with fear? I committed everything to writing and made my plan.

'Oh boy!' – Procrastination

For some reason, people are prone to procrastination. We tend to be lazy when something we don't enjoy needs to be done. Some tasks may seem so daunting that we don't even start. I have experienced this situation often and have had to force myself to get into the habit of breaking the debilitating spell. The way I did this was by the use of the expression, 'Oh boy'. It's an exclamation of joy that a child might use when you give them a gift. 'Oh boy, a model aeroplane!'

It came to me one day when I was driving to work. Another epiphany. There was a tricky intersection with no street lights and people teeming in the street. I was always tense when I got there. On that day I reframed my thoughts into, 'Oh boy, a difficult problem to solve.' When I reached that intersection, it became a challenge. And from then on, with my new attitude, I stopped dreading it.

I hate washing dishes, but as soon as I get up from the dinner table, I say to myself, 'Oh boy, clean kitchen' and I convince myself that I enjoy washing up. This simple approach works with nearly all everyday situations.

When David was young, I would say, 'Oh boy, cricket!' He would repeat, 'Oh boy, cricket' and we would go into the garden and play cricket. Or I'd say, 'Oh boy, dinner' or 'Oh boy, bath time', and it worked so well that when he had to go to school I said, 'Oh boy, school.' Luckily he also said, 'Oh boy, school.'

One of my young mentees was studying accountancy and he failed his tax exam. He told me that tax turned him to stone. I managed to convince him of the end result – that he would be getting a qualification that could be the stepping stone to success for the rest of his life. I got him to say, 'Oh boy, tax!' and 'Oh boy, degree' and on to 'Oh boy, career.' He started studying with a new enthusiasm. He passed his accountancy exam. The joke in his house became 'Oh boy, tax'.

Still today, whenever I don't feel like doing something that I know I must do, I use my 'Oh boy' technique. This often happens in the morning when I haven't slept so well and know that I should do my daily exercises. I really don't feel like it, but then I say, 'Oh boy, exercises. Oh boy, healthy body.' It works every time. It's also something like waking up in the middle of the night needing to go to the toilet. I never want to get out of bed but I know that I have to. I say to myself, 'I've got to do it sometime so I may as well do it now.' This applies to most things.

I had a difficult tax situation that I really didn't want to face. I would have done anything to avoid it, until I came up with, 'Oh boy, opportunity to put all my affairs into the most optimum state'.

I called my tax lawyer and from a potentially fraught situation we came up with a long-term solution so that there would be no more tax ambiguity.

It's easy to say 'Oh boy' when you are doing something exciting. However, it works best when there is a reluctance to do something and you need a kick.

Love Yourself!

I've always found it so difficult to love myself. I know all my imperfections. I recall making what everybody said was a brilliant speech at Roni's 60th birthday party. However, later that night, I felt disappointed because I knew that I had not made one point strongly enough about how she had handled a particularly difficult situation. Afterwards, it was all

I could think about for a day or so, even though nobody noticed it or commented on it. We demand perfection from ourselves.

Some of my most important work was to build my self-esteem. Self-esteem is different from arrogance or a feeling of superiority. It is a quiet belief in yourself and the knowledge that you are really a good person, despite your mistakes and what you think are your shortcomings. I built my self-esteem by being kind and considerate, involving myself in work, getting things done, taking even small risks and achieving small successes. When I do sometimes wander into the wilderness of debilitating self-flagellation I focus on my successes and how I have touched people's lives. The word of encouragement, the quiet compliment, shining a light for someone who's lost, the good business deal, the profitable investment, the uplifting letter, tender moments, love given and love received. I now celebrate getting 70% right instead of bemoaning the lost 30%.

When my younger son, Michael, was 11, he came home from school one day and said, 'Dad, the boys are teasing me. They say that I love myself.' I said, 'What are you supposed to do – hate yourself?' Those boys were suggesting that he was arrogant or self-centred, but it is those kinds of remarks that can cause us anxiety growing up and can last for years.

We know that we are not perfect, we all make big mistakes and we beat ourselves up terribly because of it. Our parents, our friends, our teachers, our ministers of religion, etc., in subtle ways tell us that we need to think differently, act differently or speak differently. They want us to conform to their way. This adds to our thinking that we are deficient and unworthy. As famed opera singer Aviva Pelham says of critics, 'Don't entrust your self-esteem to others. It's not safe there.'

We don't have to be arrogant or have great hubris to love ourselves. I don't think that I was ever arrogant, mainly because I never believed I had anything to be arrogant about. After struggling with the usual adolescent insecurities and being sensitive to what people would say, I came to a point of acceptance that I was a very decent person.

I had something of an epiphany in 1967 when I first saw *Fiddler on the Roof* with the great Israeli actor, Chaim Topol. There is a scene when the tailor, Motel Kamzoil, asks Tevye for his daughter's hand in marriage. As was the tradition in those days, Tevye had arranged a marriage for Tzeitel to Lazar Wolf, the wealthy, but much older, butcher. Looking down his nose, he said to Motel, 'But you're only a poor tailor.' In a rare show of defiance the usually meek and mild Motel exclaims,

'Yes, but even a poor tailor is entitled to happiness.'

At that point the scene freezes and a spotlight comes on to Tevye. He goes into deep contemplation and argues with himself, on the one hand this, on the other hand that. Eventually he decides that he can't dispute the argument. He gives approval to the match. At that defining moment, I too decided that even a relatively insecure chartered accountant was also entitled to happiness.

I felt a surge of energy come over me. I sat bolt upright in my seat. I thought, 'No more diffidence, no more doing what everyone else wants, no more caring what people might think. I will be my own person. My views count.' I walked out of the theatre with the air of someone who had just won the lottery. My date said, 'Arnie, what's come over you? I've never seen you like this.' I couldn't quite explain it to her, saying something like I was energised by the play. It was a very good night.

We have to learn to love ourselves, warts and all, and develop self-esteem.

There are numerous outstanding websites on self-compassion if you want to stop beating yourself up.

At this advanced age I can say that I do love myself – most of the time!

Kindness, Thoughtfulness and Awareness
Everyone in the world – black, white, brown, yellow, male, female, LGBT, Jewish, Muslim, Christian, Buddhist, etc., young and old, socialist and capitalist, any nationality – wants to feel good about themselves. Wherever possible, I try to make people feel good about themselves. This applies to every relationship, from the most trivial and fleeting, such as the one with the waiter at the restaurant or the shop assistant, to your deepest and most meaningful relationships with your spouse, parents, children and friends.

In Shakespeare's *The Merchant of Venice*, Act 4, Scene 1 it says, 'The quality of mercy … is twice blessed. It blesseth him that giveth and him that takes.' The same goes for making people feel good about themselves. It 'blesses' both of you.

Maya Angelou, American poet and civil rights activist, said:

'People won't always remember what you say, but they will always remember how you made them feel.'

The words you use, and your tone of voice, will determine whether you are making someone feel good about themselves and, in turn, whether they are making you feel good about yourself. They also reflect your values, concerns, desires, and character and can impact on who you are talking to, positively and negatively.

I try to treat everyone with respect, kindness and consideration. Acknowledging good service, greeting people with a smile, not hooting in the car except as a warning of danger, listening intently, not being derisory or dismissive, and not gossiping. However, I tend to treat arrogant and aggressive people with disdain and give them short thrift – in the nicest possible way of course. I try not to be arrogant and aggressive myself. I don't make myself a doormat. To paraphrase a Dr Wayne Dyer quote:

'When truth clashes with kindness, in most instances, choose kindness.'

Avoid aggressive or intimidating people, even if they are good to you. If they are nasty to others, it's only a matter of time before they will be nasty to you. A stone wrapped in chocolate is still a stone. The corollary is that you shouldn't be aggressive or intimidatory either. I was friendly with a wealthy businessman who invited Roni and me to spend a week at his villa in Tuscany. He was very hospitable and we had an enjoyable time. After we returned to Johannesburg, we went out for dinner. He intimidated the waitress to such an extent that she was in tears. I no longer wanted a friendship with this man and I ended our relationship. Not specifically, I just stopped calling him.

In order to receive love, you need to give love. Self-centredness is the antithesis of giving love. In Greek legend, Narcissus fell in love with himself when he saw his image in a clear pond. He led a lonely life, finally committing suicide.

Ask questions and try to understand how people are feeling and acknowledge those feelings before launching into how *you* are feeling. I try to use words like, 'That must have made you feel...' 'You seem particularly disappointed (or happy or confused or whatever I perceive the person to feel) ...' and they will feel understood. In his book *Between Parent and Child* (Crown Publications, revised 2003) Haim Ginott said that the most soothing thing for a child was to feel understood. It actually applies at any age. It's called active listening.

Anger, Assertiveness and Compliance

Growing up, I was a particularly compliant person. I can hardly remember an argument with my parents and I never wanted to rock the boat with my friends. It was probably out of fear of exclusion and wanting to be liked, but I'm not sure it served me well in the medium term. I was certainly well liked amongst my friends, but I was never part of the 'jocks'. I would go along with whatever my friends wanted, even when I didn't particularly want to do something. I wanted to be part of the crowd.

As I matured and learned from my mistakes, I became more assertive. When faced with tough negotiators who used bullying tactics, I would listen quietly but would use quiet strength to stay firm and assert my authority. At L&G, we had one particularly arrogant partner in a property transaction. Our partner wanted more favourable terms. I wrote to him saying that the terms would affect our returns significantly and suggested an alternative that still would have been favourable to him, but we also stood to gain. Win/win.

They wrote to our CEO and said that I was being obstructive. The CEO asked me to reply to the letter, which I did, most politely, but not moving from our position. The developers were influential in the business community and then approached the chairman. They demanded a meeting with the investment subcommittee of the board. The chairman, incorrectly in my view, called the meeting. A friend of mine had played tennis with one of the developers. He derogatorily said to my friend that I was 'just an employee' and that he would put me in my place. Imagine.

The meeting began with the developer presenting his case and being personally insulting to me. I listened quietly and patiently, saying nothing. When they had finished, the chairman asked me to respond. I produced a document that was part of the original deal 15 years previously. It was unambiguous that we were perfectly within our rights. The chairman, a highly respected lawyer, asked to see the document and showed it to the developers. The hissing sound of the air leaving their proverbial balloon was almost audible. They tried to argue that their proposal was also in the spirit of the deal and that I was ignoring that aspect.

The chairman was not swayed that we should give up our returns to a bunch of greedy and arrogant property owners. I took my alternative proposal off the table. Arnie, the employee 1. Arrogant businessmen 0. All done quietly, but clinically. The takeaway: it pays to be well prepared. Even 'only employees' deserve the utmost respect.

It was seldom that I needed to get angry and only when confronted with a business partner who tried to undermine me with other partners and company professionals, did I get extremely angry and I ruthlessly ended the partnership.

I avoid guilt-inducing and blaming statements. For instance, when Roni had an unfortunate meeting with a pillar next to our parking place, there were two possible conversations. 'How could you be so stupid? That's a new car. Do you know what that will cost? We'll lose our no claims bonus with the insurance. You really need to learn how to drive. Didn't you see the … pillar?'

Or, 'Oh gosh, Roni, you must feel so awful about this. It's not really a big thing in life. Let's call the panel beater and get it fixed. I'll let the insurance company know.'

This became a habit. I seldom raise my voice or speak in clipped tones. A soft tone offers a measure of calmness and equanimity. It is warming and comforting. It's not what you say, but how you say it. A certain way of alienating people, including your children and your parents, is to frequently raise your voice. It is very difficult to be with someone who is impatient or barks out orders like a sergeant major screaming at new recruits.

Also, nobody wants to be with someone who is always finding fault with you. Beware of getting into the habit of finding fault. This sometimes happens in long-term relationships.

There are diplomatic ways of disagreeing with someone. Instead of saying, 'You're wrong,' try something like, 'I have a different view' or 'Have you thought of this?' or 'Good thought, how about this?' 'There's a lot of truth in that, may I add this?'

Landing in Trouble

Hopefully you'll never find yourself in serious trouble. But it could happen that you have transgressed to a lesser or greater degree, depending on which rules you have broken. There are two possibilities – you have been discovered, or you have done something wrong that could be found out. If you have been found with a 'smoking gun', it may be best to confess and apologise and be prepared for the consequences. If you have done something that *could* be discovered, it's probably best to say nothing until confronted. If there is no certainty of the evidence, you have a choice – to deny or to confess. I can't really advise on this, as each case will be different, and it will be a question of your judgement. But here are some tips:

The same rules about writing things down and making a plan apply. In addition:

> ➢ You may have to accept something that will be unpleasant.
> ➢ Steel yourself to accept the worst and write down a plan of how you might deal with that.

> If your trouble isn't of a legal nature, you may need the help of a friend or relation. Decide exactly what you want to ask for and call your friend or family member and say, 'I need your help.' Just about everyone will respond positively to this.

> If it is of a legal nature, get the best lawyer you can.

Habits

The importance of habits cannot be overestimated. Your habits will define you. When I was a teenager, punctuality was for radio stations or railway stations. One day, a girl I went out with now and again got particularly angry. 'I've been waiting for half an hour, you're thoughtless and I've had enough of this. I never want to see you again.' As Churchill said, 'Never waste a good crisis.' I apologised and swore to 'NMWT' – No More Witkin Time. We drifted apart but I stuck with the habit: I am now always punctual and if I'm going to be late, I let the person know in advance. It's so easy these days. Thanks to Mr Apple, my phone can set multiple alarms!

And so it goes with many aspects of life. Your tone of voice is a habit. Good manners is a habit. Being respectful to people is a habit, as is kindness. Being controlling or demanding are habits. Defensiveness or aggression are habits. Hard work is a habit as is procrastination. Consideration (or not) of others is a habit, such as making sure that when you park you don't encroach on anyone else's parking space. Responding in a timely fashion – or not – to emails and messages is a habit. Paying bills on time is a habit, as is delaying paying bills. 'Arnie, do you realise that you are two months late with your club dues?' said the secretary of my cricket club. 'It doesn't look good and it's bad for your reputation.' I now pay every bill as soon as I get an invoice.

Awareness is the key to picking up people's feelings and sensitivities. I would observe what people found irritating in me and I would endeavour to change the habit if it wasn't fundamental to my nature. 'Arnie, are you aware that you often don't let people finish their sentences because you want to make some witty remark?' 'Thank you for that. I'll save my repartee until their sentence is finished.' You can only be yourself and can't please all of the people all of the time and shouldn't try. But when I find that I am doing things that I'm not happy with, I examine whether there is a pattern and if so I try to change it and develop a new habit. Yes, even at 76 … It never ends.

Eliminating bad habits is like getting rid of the Japanese knotweed that is strangling the plants in your garden. Developing new life-enhancing habits is like fertilising your potential.

I would recommend a book, James Clear's *Atomic Habits* (Random House Business, 2018).

Drugs

I grew up in the sixties, the height of the drug revolution. Many of my friends were smoking marijuana and there was a great deal of pressure on me to be part of the gang. The greatest pressure in the world is peer group pressure. I had taken out a girl a couple of times and rather liked her and I think the feelings were reciprocated. At a party, a friend of hers came up to us and asked her if she was coming to smoke a joint. I was quite surprised, because this hadn't come up before. She saw my expression and invited me to join in. 'C'mon, Arnie, everybody does it. You'll be floating on cloud nine. You really are missing out. You don't want to be an outsider. Don't be such a square.'

Defining moment. Beautiful girl whom I'm trying to impress. Most of my friends are doing it. The promise of something more after the drugs. Maybe it isn't so bad after all. My inner voice telling me it's the start of a slippery slope into addiction.

Fortunately, common sense prevailed. I said,

'You either like lettuce or you don't. I don't like the thought of doing drugs.'

I don't eat lettuce simply because I don't like it. That is one line that nobody can argue with. It can't be 'wrong' or 'right' to like something or not. It sounds simple but it became one of my paradigms. The loss of a potential girlfriend was a cheap price to pay.

There is a phenomenon called the social justification of decision-making. People like to justify their decisions. For instance, somebody buys a Ford car and they tell everybody that it is the only car to buy, much better than a Mercedes Benz, an Audi or a Vauxhall. It is the same with drugs.

My suggestion is to never, *ever* take drugs (excluding prescribed medicine):

> ➤ Don't experiment.
> ➤ Never bow to peer group pressure.
> ➤ Never think it's glamorous just because pop stars and movie stars tell of their exploits and make it look appealing.
> ➤ One small, apparently harmless, experiment can be the first step to destruction.
> ➤ Drugs kill.

- Drugs cloud judgement.
- Drugs create addicts.
- Addicts create misery for themselves.
- Addicts create misery for the community.

Addiction starts with one tiny step. One tiny step can be the start of a difficult lifelong journey – a journey from which there may be no return.

Gambling

Gambling is a form of drug. It can be overwhelmingly addictive. It works on the basis of 'intermittent reinforcement'. This was a term coined by the behavioural psychologist B.F. Skinner. Put simply, it is reward for an action that takes place when you don't know when it will happen.

Think of a food you really enjoy. If you had it for breakfast, lunch and supper every day you would soon tire of it. If your boyfriend/ girlfriend/partner/friend told you every hour how wonderful you are, it would lose meaning. If they criticised you on a continual basis you would soon get out of the relationship. However, if they occasionally and randomly gave you a compliment, you will always be waiting for the next affirmation. According to Skinner, when applied in the workplace, the worker will always be trying to do his/her best at all times because they don't know when the next feedback will come. Their behaviour will be addictive.

You put money on the roulette wheel and every now and again your number comes up. You don't know when, but it is a great thrill when it does. Slot machines are programmed so that the player will win every now and again. Players think, 'I can do this. I can win.' That moves them to keep playing and, unless they're very disciplined and stop, they will play until they run out of money or until the casino closes.

Roni and I used to enjoy going to the casino now and again. We always had a money limit and a time limit. We were rational. Over the years, we probably broke about even. Today it's more difficult, but all the more important, to be disciplined with online casinos being open 24/7.

I know the dangers of gambling – I worked for a casino – The London Playboy Club.

One night in around 1990, we lost our discipline, exceeded our limit and played on for too long. I decided there and then that I would stop gambling and I did. We did go back to a casino now and again when invited. Having once been good clients, the casino tried to entice us back with a 'gift' of £1,000 in chips. We went, won £8,000, and never went back!

Not so lucky was a friend of ours who got really hooked. He lost all his money and had a family to support. He committed suicide. My uncle was addicted to betting on horses in the thirties and forties. He ended up in a council flat in Waterloo, supported by my father and another uncle.

I'm not saying that you shouldn't enjoy a flutter every now and again, if that's your thing. Just notice how much you are doing it. Danger signals are always flashing. Heed them.

Gossip

Two friends are discussing one of their other friends:

Marvin: 'Did you hear that Roger didn't get the promotion he thought he would? I'm not surprised. He thinks he's so smart, but he's really quite a shallow person. When we were in Florida on holiday he was always trying to impress the girls with his knowledge. I knew that it was rather superficial, but he succeeded now and again.'

Colin: 'I think that Roger is very astute. As I understand it, the promotion was because the firm decided that all staff movements were frozen for a year as a result of the coronavirus. He has a very nice girlfriend now, so I guess she thinks that he's okay.'

Who would you rather have as your friend? Since everything reflects on the person doing the saying, the chances are that Marvin is a bit jealous or envious of Roger. Perhaps he really is more successful with girls than Marvin. Colin may remain friendly with Marvin, but can he ever really trust him not to speak badly about him?

Colin on the other hand is a loyal friend and should be cherished by both Roger and Marvin.

Of course, we all talk about people and there is nothing wrong with that. We are interested in what our friends or acquaintances are doing and that is most natural. It's what you say and how you say it that is important. It can be kind and understanding or nasty and deliberately intended to hurt.

The motivation for gossip is often to make ourselves appear 'in the know'. We think that it may elevate us and to some extent give us a feeling of 'superiority', especially if the gossip reflects badly on the person being talked about. If you are aware that this is your motivation, it may prevent you from harmful gossip.

Idle gossip is destructive to both the person doing the saying and the person being spoken about. When you consciously talk ill of someone, you are ingesting a little bit of that poison.

In Proverbs, it says, 'Life and death are in the power of the tongue.' One malicious sentence can end a relationship. One nurturing sentence can cement a relationship.

Judgement

There is a difference between being judgemental and using your judgement. Being judgemental of someone's way of life may be pejorative. Using your judgement about whether to mix with them or not is vital. Success or failure in life will be determined by the judgements you make. Before making a judgement, you need to have as much information as possible. Sometimes we make snap judgements about people, particularly love interests. That may be fine, but before entering into any long-term relationship, both personal and business, it is best to find out as much as you can about the person/people you are getting involved with.

Being judgemental of someone or their actions can be stifling. 'Why would you want to go hiking for seven days? It's just a waste of time.' 'Give up your fantasy about wanting to make it in Hollywood.' 'That make-up is unsuitable for a 16-year-old.' These are all judgemental statements without understanding the motivation of the other person. They can be damaging, depending on how they're taken.

I believe that I am very non-judgemental. That's why so many people confide in me. I will always ask them questions. Questions shine a light on where they may be headed. I will never make someone feel foolish about what they are doing or their plans and dreams.

However, I will most certainly exercise my judgement every time as to who I mix with and what behaviour is acceptable to me on a personal level.

When I was the investment manager of L&G, we did a lot of business on the stock exchange. I was sought after by the stockbroking community but decided that we would use only four stockbrokers. Some of the financial institutions which were much larger than we were had up to 20 stockbrokers that they dealt with. Other broking firms were always trying to get our business and one such broker invited me to his private game farm. These private game farms were very exclusive and out of reach of institutional dealers. I would have had to spend a whole weekend with the broker. I wasn't judgemental of his agenda but my judgement told me that if I went, I would be indebted to him forever. I refused that time and the other four times he asked me.

Decisions can be life-changing, for the good and the not so good. It takes 25 years to build a reputation and 25 seconds to destroy it with a bad judgement. Examples are experimenting with drugs or making a racist statement or consorting with crooks or paedophiles.

Chapter 2

Relationships

Parents

I was extremely lucky. I don't recall ever having an argument with my parents. Maybe I was just naturally respectful or maybe I was just the kind of person who stayed on the straight and narrow and did what I was told. My parents never nagged me to work harder or to do my homework. If I did badly, it was my fault and I had to bear the consequences. My parents were always receptive to what I wanted to do and did everything they could to help me. When I was 18, they gave me the full use of my mother's car.

I was very close to my parents, but never shared my inner thoughts, feelings and insecurities with them. I'm sure they would have been sympathetic but I felt I needed to handle things myself. My mother was very anxious about most things. She occasionally warned me to be careful of certain people, which I ignored. However she never became insistent or admonishing. My father was also very understanding and kind and did not try to control me. I guess if I wanted to do something dangerous or completely inappropriate, he would have said something.

This was in contrast to my parents' relationships with my brother and sister who both pushed boundaries excessively and caused them a great deal of grief. By observing these difficult relationships, I think I realised that I had to be the 'good one'. This could explain why I never argued with my parents or why they left me to do my own thing.

From a young age my brother was in continual trouble. My father was constantly bailing him out and this continued until my father died. My sister had emotional problems which my parents struggled with. Between my brother and sister, my parents did not have a day without tension.

One of the most difficult things in the world is to see your children suffer. The second most difficult is to see your parents suffer.

Understand your parents' concern and respect their sensitivities. Speak in a respectful tone of voice even if arguing a point where you disagree. Put your case rationally and sensibly and you will likely get your way. 'Mom, I know that you are concerned that I may get into trouble if I stay out too late, but I promise you I am responsible.' 'Dad, I know that you think that that boy just wants one thing, but I can assure you that he is trustworthy.' The one area of concern for my parents was the time I would be returning home. I would usually give myself a wide berth (saying it would be later than I intended) so that I did not disappoint them.

By all means have disagreements with your parents, especially when you are in their home. However, never raise your voice or be aggressive or rude. At all times be respectful. If you can't get your own way, when you are independent you can do what you like.

If your parents are really abusive and beat you, see someone that you can trust or seek out social services or other recognised helplines. Never tolerate physical violence or emotional abuse from a parent – or from anyone else.

Parents can sometimes have demands or expectations that you won't do certain things, but very often it is a reflection of their own insecurity. For instance, when I was 18, I had a friend whose parents' demands were irrational – such as 'I forbid you to mix with Black or Chinese people'. This was, after all, apartheid South Africa. It only said something about their phobias and prejudices. We were friendly with a Chinese guy and he ignored his parents' exhortations. He just did it without them knowing. We agreed that if they found out, he would be honest and tell them, in a calm voice, that he had done nothing wrong. If he were punished, he would accept the punishment, but it wouldn't stop him doing things that weren't wrong or dangerous.

I was always loving to my parents and would tell them that I loved them. My father was bald and for all of his life I used to kiss him on his forehead whenever I saw him and say, 'Good to see you, dad.' 'You too, Arnie boy,' was his response.

When I left home at age 21, my relationship with my parents changed completely. I was an independent man and, although they still had lots of concerns and 'advice', the relationship was more 'adult to adult'. Know that your parents will always worry about you and you about them, especially as they get older. Try to base your relationship on mutual respect, admiration and love.

In 1996, I was in Johannesburg on business. At three in the morning my pleasant dream was shattered by the shrill ring of the telephone. I fumbled in the dark, heart racing. My first thought was that something terrible had happened. 'Hi, Dad,' my son David said. 'Nothing's wrong. I couldn't sleep.' All within the space of a few seconds my thought process was, 'If nothing's wrong, why the hell did you call me at three in the morning? If you can't sleep do you have to wake me up when I've got a busy day tomorrow?' What I did say was, 'Davey, something must be very important for you to call me at this time. What is it, son?' 'I have an exam tomorrow and I can't fall asleep.' 'Okay,' I said, 'Put your phone on speaker and I'll take you through the yoga "death pose".'

This is an exercise where you lie on your back, palms facing upwards. You tense all your muscles and then let go. You then focus your attention on each part of your body and relax it, starting with your feet, moving to your calves, thighs, torso and up to the head. I talked him through it and after about five minutes he said that he was falling asleep and the phone clicked off.

He did very well in the exam.

For him to call me at three in the morning showed a huge amount of mutual respect. He knew that I wouldn't get angry and that I would understand. I actually felt quite delighted because it affirmed for me that I wasn't such a bad father. It showed the closeness and trust between us, which is how relationships with parents should be.

More recently, Michael also called me at two in the morning. Seems that I'm destined to be woken up by my children. I'm assuming that this will happen soon with my grandchildren.

I think that one's relationship with one's parents can be summed up by what Michael said to me a couple of years ago. 'Dad,' he said, 'It's so very difficult being a parent. Only now do I realise what great parents you were. Sorry if I gave you a tough time.'

Being a Parent

When the time comes for you to be parent, you'll discover that it's just about the most difficult job you will ever have. When it happens, I suggest that you buy books on parenting and read them carefully. Unfortunately, it is not a school or university subject. I will offer just one suggestion that formed the basis of my relationships with my children.

The first rule is to recognise their feelings, repeat them and show that you understand.

'That must have felt …'
'You seem very hurt about …'
'You wanted revenge …'

My grandson, age 12, is a vegetarian and a very picky eater. He had continual battles with his parents about his food and almost every mealtime was filled with tension. He and Michael were visiting us and there was a big fight about what he would eat. Michael 'lost it' and shouted at him. He came into my study sobbing.

'Ansel, you seem very hurt,' I said. 'What is worrying you?'

'My parents are always on at me about my food and they don't understand that I don't like things,' he answered.

'That must be very frustrating,' I said. 'Tell me, what is it that you do like?'

He proceeded to go through all his likes such as pasta, oats, tofu, rice, ice cream, and more. It ran to nearly three pages. I printed it out for him and emailed a copy to his parents. He was very excited. I said that he needed to tell his parents what he wanted for dinner before he went to school. That way, there could never be any arguments about food again. Ansel is not a particularly demonstrative child, but he tilted his head and looked at me lovingly. Much to my surprise he came around my desk and gave me a big hug and held on to me. 'Thank you, Grandpa, I love you.' There have been no more arguments over food.

- First-time parents get no handbooks on how to parent. They have no experience doing it.
- My best suggestion for raising children is to remember how your parents treated you and try to bring the positive aspects of how you were parented into your own parenting.
- You may not have liked what your parents said or did in certain instances, but you may recognise (in hindsight) that what they said was important or made sense.
- Whatever you didn't like, make sure you don't do that to your children.
- When new situations arise remember that children (and all people) want to feel good about themselves.
- When they do something that is likely to make them feel bad about themselves, you need to be kind and separate the behaviour from the child.
- You still need to be firm, especially if the behaviour is potentially dangerous to them. 'That is something that shouldn't be repeated for the following reasons ...' 'Do you understand how what you did could ...?' 'I love you.'
- Children need and appreciate boundaries. That gives them a sense of right and wrong and helps them develop appropriate behaviour.
- Respect your children's privacy – remember how you wanted privacy.

Siblings

Sibling rivalry is the oldest conflict in the world. Think of Cain and Abel, or Jacob and Esau. The question is, whether this is the natural order of things and, if so, how can we make our relationships with our siblings more fulfilling?

Because my relationship with my siblings was so fraught, I find it difficult to make many comments. In 1975, I verbalised that I never wanted to speak to my brother again. The main reason was that I was afraid that if I had any relationship with him I would have been dragged into his black hole. It was more self-preservation than enmity.

Similarly, I had difficulties with my sister. I felt powerless to help her and I was being sucked into her abyss. I sometimes feel guilty that I wasn't able to do more.

At my 60th birthday party, my very good friend's mother said that he and I were like brothers. I said, 'I hope that we're closer than that!'

Roni is an only child, thus had no problem with sibling rivalry.

When we are very young, it is difficult to understand the dynamic of having to share our parents' love with others. The feelings of a first child have been described as follows: It's like your husband (or wife) saying that he/she is taking a second spouse, 'but don't worry I won't love you any less. My new spouse will move down the hall and I will be spending a great deal of time with him/her, but you will always be just as important to me as ever.'

Even with the greatest preparation and show of affection, the first child – and subsequent children – are likely to have feelings of jealousy and anger. These can take many years to overcome. By the time you are a teenager, with more of an ability to deal with complex emotions, you are likely to negotiate these feelings and normalise your relationship. If you are lucky, you will have a close relationship with your siblings. Value them.

It seems to me that, although the relationship is different from all others, the general principles of all relationships still apply.

- ➤ Think of your siblings as you would a friend and apply the same criteria.
- ➤ Try to make them feel good about themselves – it will also make you feel good.
- ➤ If you have them, recognise your feelings of jealousy or envy.
- ➤ Force yourself to at least express appreciation of their achievements – if you can't beat them, join them.
- ➤ If they have problems, be sympathetic and try to help as best you can.
- ➤ If the relationship is really toxic with little possibility of being 'normal', distance yourself. On the occasions that you are together

– family functions – be polite. You owe it to the people who are there not to make a scene.

Grandparents

I only had one surviving grandparent and he was a distant, reserved man, so I never had the opportunity of being able to talk freely to him or learn from his wisdom. Roni and I are very close to our grandchildren. Most of them actually seek our company. My grandson, Ari, said to David, 'Dad, you are so lucky that you have such wonderful parents.' When he told me this I said, 'Ari, so are you.'

I don't have much practical experience of being a grandchild but these are my thoughts.

➢ Treat your grandparents with respect. Pay attention to them: older people often feel 'invisible' to younger people. My heart leaps when I get a WhatsApp message from any of my grandchildren and I hear, 'Hi, Grandpa, just called to see how you are doing.'

➢ Grandparents have a wealth of experience that you can tap into and benefit from. Talk to them. Ask them questions.

➢ Grandparents can be annoying by describing how things were 'in their day'. Be kind and humour them – they only want the best for you. By all means debate with them.

➢ There may be an impasse with your parents which your grandparents can help resolve. Your grandparents are usually able to take a neutral position and examine the facts, without the emotion that parents and children tend to bring to the situation.

➢ Visit your grandparents!

➢ Tell your grandparents that you love them: even very old people want to feel loved. In fact, the older they get, the more they want to feel loved.

➢ Kind words from a grandchild are like an adrenaline shot to a grandparent's soul.

Friends

My first recollection of friends is from nursery school. I went to Oxford Nursery School and I clearly remember playdates with a number of my friends. We lived in Flint Road in Parkwood and my first two years of school were at Parkview Junior School. I used to get a lift from Mervyn Cohen's father. The Cohens lived three blocks from us and I can clearly recall walking to their house at age five, crossing Jan Smuts Avenue, which was a busy thoroughfare. Our other friend was David Mordant, who lived much closer. We were always at each other's homes, frequently sleeping over. This was when I was six years old.

After two years at Parkview, we moved to Saxonwold School and there I made a number of new friends. I went on playdates almost every day after school. My friends became my family.

I found it easy to relate and was always kind and considerate. I seldom had disagreements, possibly because I was not particularly demanding. I was prepared to put up with barbs to maintain the relationships. Even when I was obese and occasionally teased, my friendships didn't fade.

Never speak badly about your friends behind their backs. I try never to speak badly about *anybody* behind their back. I sometimes don't succeed, especially if I think that a person is really not a good person. To me loyalty means that if someone speaks badly about my friend, I need to defend the friend.

When I was about 16, I said something mildly derogatory about a friend who wasn't that close but was part of our 'crew'. Unthinkingly, the boy I said it to reported it to him. The friend challenged me and aggressively said that if I had anything to say about him, I should say it straight to his face. I was shocked by the rebuke, but it was one of the most valuable lessons I have ever learnt. 'If an error is corrected ...'

I can say with certainty that I am a very good friend. I have a great many close friends all over the world. People confide intimate details of their lives, knowing that I won't judge them or repeat what I hear. I am always on my friends' side and wish them well. Of course, sometimes a little envy emerges, which is natural, but it never lasts for more than a few minutes.

When I don't like someone (which is rare) or when someone just doesn't interest me, I am always polite but don't waste time with them.

There are lots of reasons for being a friend, but probably the most important is that the person makes you feel good about yourself and you make them feel good about themselves.

The Meaning of Friendship

There are various depths of friendship – not everyone is your 'best friend'. There are acquaintances who are fun to be with occasionally. Sometimes you have friends because they are interesting or you share a hobby such as golf or bridge or hiking or quilting.

Don't expect or demand anything from your friends. Friendship is give and take by both parties. Not I give and you take. Beware of people who only take, even if they are 'popular' or 'attractive'.

You can often tell a person's character by even the smallest of actions. Everything is a microcosm of everything else. Someone gets out of his car in a parking garage and notices that he has parked too close to the line. If he gets back into the car to move it, he is likely to be considerate in most other ways. A large tip to a waiter would indicate generosity at all levels and someone who operates in an atmosphere of abundance. Impatient carping to service people suggests the person is quite self-centred and needs you to do things for them. I like being with people who do 'random acts of kindness.'

By listening carefully, you can understand what the other person is thinking and feeling ('listen' and 'silent' are an anagram of each other).

Very often people put on a 'front.' When I was about 18, a girl said to me that I had a 'front' of nonchalance. This was not a compliment. Generally, you should just be yourself, but if you must put on a front, let it be a front of kindness. If you aren't yourself, then, in theory, it doesn't matter what front you put on. So, if you really don't feel kind, at least the 'front' of kindness will make the other person feel good.

One day (in 1968 before the advent of cell phones!) I arranged to meet a friend at the corner of Eloff and Commissioner Streets in Johannesburg at 1pm. When he hadn't turned up by 1.20pm, I left. Should I have been annoyed? I don't think so. If he had been in an accident, I couldn't be angry. If something extremely important had come up at work, I couldn't be angry. If he had simply forgotten and didn't do it on purpose, I couldn't be angry. When I returned to my office I called him to see if he was OK. He was most apologetic. He had written in the wrong day in his diary. Had he not been apologetic, or if he had done it maliciously, I would have ended the friendship.

None of us is perfect and we remain friends with people despite their flaws and ours. Without this acceptance, there would never be any relationships. However, anyone who can be deliberately malicious, even if not to you, isn't worth wasting time on. Be vigilant and avoid malicious or nasty people, no matter how 'rich' or 'exciting' or 'sexy' they seem.

Somebody can *give* offence, but you don't have to *take* offence. I had an acquaintance (I won't call him a friend) who wrote an article in a blog which I considered racist. I wrote to him and asked him to take me off his mailing list. He apologised for offending me. I replied:

'You're not important enough to offend me. Can a mouse offend an elephant? A turd on the side of the road is potentially offensive, but it is still a turd that I will avoid.'

Be loyal to your friends, but not if that loyalty is misplaced. For instance, if your friend has committed a crime or done something dishonourable and wants to make you an accessory to it, do not do it. It would be the same as if you had committed that crime or done the dishonourable thing. You could be left with unpleasant consequences. A good friend would never ask you to perjure yourself or put yourself in danger in order to cover their misdeeds.

A friend, whom I'll call Tom, once used my name as a reference for a position, without asking me. He claimed that he had had run a company in India that I knew to be untrue. I was in an invidious position. If I confirmed his claims and he was later discovered, which almost certainly would have happened when his CV was checked, I would have been tarred with the same deceptive brush. My reputation was in jeopardy. The chairman called me to discuss the application.

It would have been easy for me to expose him, in order to protect myself. That could have been very damaging to him. I said that Tom was a wonderful person and would be a credit to any organisation. I said that I thought that he wouldn't be suited for that particular position. I did not mention the fabricated business experience and fortunately I wasn't asked about it. Had I been asked I would have been forced to say that I knew nothing about it. Tom was particularly lucky that the chairman agreed with me. The worst possible outcome was that he would have been considered for the position. His reputation would have been in tatters.

Tom had potentially impugned my credibility by suggesting that I endorsed his application. He should have known perfectly well that I would never perjure myself. He *expected* me to abandon my principles. I'm proud of the fact that I didn't expose him and that I deflected the conversation. I saved his reputation, at the same time as maintaining my integrity and credibility. The organisation was left with a very favourable impression of Tom.

I should have excommunicated him. Most people would have. However, the burial service says, 'There are none righteous on earth who doeth only good and sinneth not.' I was ready to forgive him. Astonishingly, he blamed me for not being more forceful with the chairman on his behalf. He excommunicated me! I am not at all upset about it. 'No good deed goes unpunished.'

Demonstrate meaningful gestures of friendship if you can. When I was diagnosed with my first cancer, a good friend in the US commissioned a 100 page report on thyroid cancer from Johns Hopkins University. It was so unexpected and I was so grateful. It gave me great insight into the possibilities for treatment.

When a friend was diagnosed with incurable cancer in Johannesburg seven years ago, Roni and I flew from London to say goodbye to him. He was overwhelmed with gratitude, as were his family. He died a few days later and one could say that it made no difference whether we were there or not. However, we gave him solace in his last days and we felt good about it as well. We did what we thought was right.

Friendships can span decades – I have been close friends with five or six people for more than 60 years. Friendships change and people grow apart; accept it. Just because you have a 'history' with someone doesn't mean you have to continue being their friend. I had a flatmate who was always taking advantage of me and giving very little back. I was responsible for letting it happen for nearly 40 years until I decided that I would not contact him again. He had fallen on relatively hard times, had very few friends and was apparently not very happy. Roni tried to encourage me to contact him again because we had a 'history' but I declined. She thought it was quite heartless.

A bad reason for staying friends with someone is out of pity. It diminishes the person being 'pitied'. That doesn't mean that you shouldn't befriend someone with a disability, for example. It may be a kind thing to do, as long as you treat them as equals. But it is not obligatory – that person may simply not be your type of person.

Try to avoid lending or borrowing money unless it is for something very specific, you know the boundaries, and you are sure you will be able to pay them back or vice versa. Better to give someone money than to lend it to them if they are likely to have a problem paying it back. 'Touch a man's pocket and you touch his soul.'

Energy
Life is energy. For me, the very best reason to be with someone is because they give me energy and don't drain energy from me. This applies to all relationships. People who complain or who indulge in self-pity or are demanding and have high expectations can contaminate the atmosphere and drain energy.

If I feel my energy being drained, I move on. The converse is true – I am aware that I need to give energy, not drain it. I usually do this by having a positive attitude and not bemoaning my fate. People tend to respond to hopeful language and avoid harbingers of doom.

I used to do yoga and one day the yoga teacher asked me how I was. I said I was fine. He said, 'What do you mean "fine"? You must be wonderful, super-wonderful, hyper-super-wonderful.' After that, when people asked me how I was, I used to answer, 'Wonderful' or 'Tickety boo'. When I responded like that I always felt better, no matter how I was really feeling. It also gave energy to the other person, because it was positive. One of my friends used to call me Mr Wonderful. I was perceived to be someone who looked for solutions and therefore many people would consult me and seek my company. People seemed pleased to see me. When I meet people I usually am glad to see them, whatever I'm feeling. Just the meeting, in itself, makes me feel good.

When both people give energy, both are elevated. You don't have to be a Pollyanna, always full of sweetness and light. You can still have strong views and differences of opinion that can be expressed forcibly without being offensive or personal, except on the rare occasions when you need to be.

Do not allow yourself to disappear into someone else's 'black hole', especially if it's very black. My mother-in-law, Musia, could never emotionally leave the concentration camp, Dachau, where she'd been imprisoned during the Second World War. Indeed, nothing could be worse than what she endured. I was extremely sensitive to her situation and tried to be as accommodating as possible. However, it was important for me to keep my energy up and not be totally drawn into her depression.

From a very young age, Roni always focussed on the now and the need to move on and develop. She, too, was empathetic to her mother, but wouldn't be drawn into the black hole. Strangely enough, it was her mother's adversity that made Roni so strong. She had to carry her mother from around the age of 12. As Shakespeare said in *As You Like It* (Act 2, Scene 1), 'Sweet are the uses of adversity.'

Musia had struggled all her life. To make ends meet, she took on four teaching jobs, starting at 7am and ending at 9pm. She lived in a modest apartment. On her 70th birthday, Roni made a grand party for her. The mouth-watering food was supplied by a celebrity chef, Roni splashed out on a glamorous outfit for her and she had her hair beautifully coiffured.

One of her pupils spoke of the intimacy of the lessons. It was more like group therapy in the guise of learning Hebrew. He said that she was adored by everyone who knew her.

Musia told me that it was the first birthday party she had had since she was 15 when she was taken to the concentration camp.

At the end of the emotional evening I asked her, 'Musia, did you enjoy your party?' 'Well,' she said, 'when I think of what they did to my father and brother in the camps, how can I enjoy myself?' They were both killed.

Sometimes, friends go through a very traumatic experience and are in a deep black hole. One of my best friends lost a son in an accident. I felt it was important to be strong for them, empathetic and to stand by them, even if it meant a temporary drain on my energy, for many months and even years. It's only when someone is in a permanent depression that, at some point, you might need to move on.

The Importance of Letter Writing

In 1987, a friend of mine emigrated to Australia with his wife and family. About three years later, I heard that he was having a rough time. He had a problem with his partners in a financial services business and they had ousted him. He had been prominent in South Africa but was not well known in Sydney.

I wrote him a letter (there were no emails). I said how I understood his plight and that I was sorry. I reminded him that he had been successful in South Africa and I emphasised four of the most important words in the English language, 'I believe in you.' I also quoted:

'When a diamond falls into the mud, it's still a diamond. When dust rises to heaven it's still dust.'

Many years later, for my 60th birthday, Roni asked a number of my friends to write a message that she included in a 'birthday book'. His contribution was about the dramatic effect of my letter on him. He had received it at a very low point in his life, when he had lost his self-esteem.

When he read that I believed in him, it had been a wake-up call. He drew on his previous experience, started a new business and at the time of my birthday, was again riding high. He said that he carried that letter in his briefcase and referred to it when he wasn't feeling great. On my 70th birthday he wrote again to say that after 25 years he still referred to the letter. He said that it was somewhat faded, but the message was as fresh as ever.

In 2002, the Chief Rabbi of the UK, Jonathan Sacks, wrote a book called *The Dignity of Difference* (Continuum). In it, he said that all religions had their gods and we should respect that. The ultra-orthodox Jewish movement in the UK were outraged. They contended that there was only one God and they wanted the Chief Rabbi impeached. Around that time, he gave an interview to the *Guardian*, a left wing newspaper who reviewed the book. The interviewer asked him whether he had sympathy for the Palestinians who had died in the conflict. He replied that he wept for all innocent people who were casualties of the conflict. The headline in the *Guardian* went something like, 'Chief Rabbi criticises Israel'. This was not the case, but it hurt the Chief Rabbi.

My friend who knew Rabbi Sacks well told me that he was quite depressed about the outcome. I wrote him a letter. I had never met him. I had heard him make a speech about Israel a year earlier, the theme of which was 'Israel, I'm proud of you'. The theme of my letter was 'Jonathan Sacks, I'm proud of you.' It was a two-page letter, with that phrase used intermittently. A short while later he wrote to me. 'Words cannot express the thanks I feel for your profound and encouraging letter,' he said. 'I cherish it as one of the most moving letters I have ever received.'

Three years later I met him at a function. I went up to him and introduced myself. I said, 'I'm Arnie Witkin. I wrote you a letter.' He said, 'I remember it well. I filed it in my "Good News" file. Whenever I get a bit low, I open the file and page through it. It contains letters and articles that make me feel good. Thank you again for your letter.'

I was quite astonished that a man of God would have something as worldly as a 'Good News' file. He has at his disposal thousands of references that could bring him comfort. He was as human as everybody else. Very sadly he died from cancer recently.

Another friend's business went bankrupt. I wrote him a letter telling him how sorry I was and that he was still a wonderful person. I told him how my father had gone broke but had retained his dignity. My friend cleared everything off the one wall of his office and hung my framed letter. He told me that in the depths of his crisis, my letter reminded him that just because he had lost his business, he was still valued as a person. After a while he got back on his feet, but the letter remained on the wall.

I have written to friends who were having operations and given them encouragement and a process for handling the situation. My one friend who had a particularly aggressive cancer said that one of my letters kept him going through the chemotherapy treatment. I have written letters to my wife and children that they say moved them and that they will keep forever. I always write a note after going to friends for dinner. My friends always appreciate a note on their birthdays or other special occasions.

The written word means a lot. Write letters to important people and to less important people. It is always appreciated. Also, keep meaningful letters that you receive. You will get a great deal of joy in later years reading them. I wish I had kept some of the letters I received.

Romantic Relationships
Renowned British poet, John Keats, said:

> *'I am certain of nothing but the holiness of the heart's affection and the truth of imagination.'*

(Also see Chapter 3)

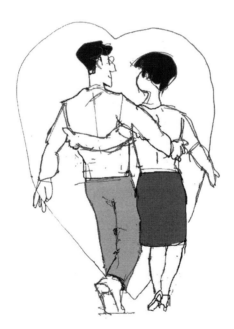

In my paradigm, love is one of the three legs of the three-legged stool that supports a balanced life. A Venn diagram consists of three interlocking circles. Imagine each circle is called 'Body', 'Mind' and 'Spirit'. They all come together in the centre. I'm calling that love between a man and woman or between two adults of the same sex in a romantic relationship.

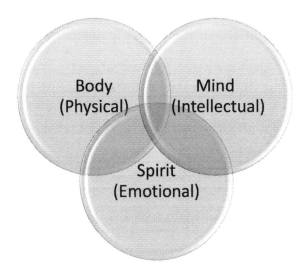

Where the circles all meet, there is compatibility, maybe even 'The One'.

It is very easy for bodies to come together, even for one night. Equally, it is easy to be intellectually compatible with someone who has similar interests. Sometimes you can have both together. For 'Spirit', read values, interests, wanting to make each other feel good and comfortable, with no controlling or abusive behaviour. When you have all three that meet in the centre of the diagram that's compatibility and may be your 'true love.' That person could be 'The One'.

The surest way to feel good about yourself is to feel loved and be able to express love, especially in a deep relationship with someone. And yet, that love relationship is often one of the most complicated and fraught of all. It involves total commitment and an abandonment of your external shields and masks.

I found that my relationships with girls (and women) were quite difficult. Growing up, I was overweight and therefore extremely self-conscious. Although I had an interest in girls, I was certainly far too shy to approach them. When I was in Grade 7, age 13, one of the girls had a batmitzvah party – boys and girls – with dancing. When my parents came to pick me up, they found me eating a hot dog. My father laughed with my mother and said he'd thought that that's where he'd find me. I was actually afraid of rejection and didn't have the courage to ask anyone to dance.

There are many reasons for having a relationship. Possibly the best reason is that someone is interesting and attractive to you, and you are more or less at the same intellectual level. When there is a big gap in intellect, the relationship may be intensely physical for a while, but in the long term it's unlikely to last. What do you talk about, especially in company when one party doesn't participate or says something inappropriate?

It is a priceless gift to be with someone who makes you laugh and who you make laugh (or at least appreciate their sense of humour). Love is laughing at your partner's jokes and stories over and over again. You're very unlikely to laugh at the joke of someone you dislike. In all relationships, the first thing that you have to do is establish rapport. Here are some of the ways that I found useful:

- ➢ Ask relevant, unthreatening questions.
- ➢ Be a good listener.
- ➢ Understand how the other person is feeling. This is empathy.
- ➢ Be non-judgemental.
- ➢ Establish eye contact.
- ➢ Discover shared values and passions.
- ➢ Recognise that the other person may be shy and make them feel at ease. In the book *Cat's Cradle* by Kurt Vonnegut, the most beautiful girl in the world, Mona, meets the hero of the book, who is described as very reticent and quite awkward. Recognising his diffidence, she greets him with the greeting for shy people, 'You can make no mistake.'
- ➢ If you can find something humorous to say, especially if it is self-deprecating, it will break the ice quickly.

Sympathy or fear that you will hurt the other person if you break up are the worst reasons for having a relationship. They are responsible for themselves. Breaking off a relationship may be the best thing for you and them.

Good reasons for a relationship are shared values, you can laugh at each other's jokes, you make each other feel good about yourselves and you are physically compatible.

If a relationship is a bit rocky your partner may say that nobody will ever love you more than they do. This is a poor reason to stay in a bad relationship. Consider dumping them immediately. Plenty of people will love you just as much, if not more. If someone says that they will kill themselves, or kill you, if you break up with them, walk away and do not see them again. That kind of blackmail will keep you a slave forever. If they do kill themselves (as has happened), it's not your fault. They are responsible for themselves; you absolutely did the right thing.

If someone insists that you give up something that is important to you because they don't like it, my advice to you is to dump them immediately. They will control you forever and stifle you and your creativity. If a sport is very important to you and you play every weekend, but your partner asks that you give it up or she/he will break up with you, get out as fast as you can. There is a strong likelihood that if you comply and end up marrying the person, you could have resentment for life – strange as it may sound. A few years ago, I was at a dinner party and sat next to a woman who was a ballroom dancer in her younger days. Her fiancé, who was clearly insecure, didn't want her to be in close proximity to other men and insisted that she give up dancing. She reluctantly agreed. She told me that she still regretted it and always wondered whether she could have had a dancing career.

I played cricket until I was 61 years old. When I met Roni, I used to play every Saturday and Sunday. It was important to me. I'm not certain exactly what Roni felt, but she encouraged it. In fact, when David was born she used to bring him to the games in his carry cot and score for us. She also sometimes made tea for the teams. If you can't beat them, join them. I probably would never have stayed married, or got married, had she objected. Fortunately we'll never know!

Love is letting go completely and making yourself vulnerable to the other person. If you're hurt, so be it. There are always many more prospective partners.

Strength, money, power, confidence (without arrogance) and position are very attractive to both women and men. If those qualities come with control levers and strings attached, beware. You don't want to end up like a bird in a gilded cage.

Strength

What does strength mean? It involves:

➤ A quiet belief in yourself.
➤ A sense of dignity.
➤ A strong set of values.
➤ The ability to be decisive.
➤ It is doing what you think is right and not doing what you think is wrong.
➤ It is being independent and not needy.
➤ Strength is not necessarily physical muscle or a domineering

personality. Behaving in a domineering way may actually be a sign of insecurity, showing a need to be in control.

➢ Weakness is unappealing.

➢ Kindness of any sort can be extremely sexy. People are attracted to kind people, but usually not if they're weak.

➢ As Kahlil Gibran wrote in *The Prophet*, 'Tenderness and kindness are not signs of weakness and despair, but manifestations of strength and resolution.'

➢ The ultimate aphrodisiac is strength combined with compassion and kindness.

➢ Politeness and good manners are equally attractive. To verify this, just observe people who are polite and well-mannered and those who are boorish and uncouth, and decide which you like better.

➢ Swearing falls into the category of being uncouth, but there are occasions when it can be funny or appropriate, for instance, when it's reported speech or if it's necessary in a joke. I very seldom swear and certainly not in public. A friend said that it was not natural, so I said, 'The worst word I use is "bloody" and that's f*** all.' I think that that was funny and appropriate.

➢ It's best not to be a prude and castigate someone if they swear, unless it really is gratuitously crude and offensive.

➢ No relationship is perfect; there will be things about your partner that you may not like and can't change. Strength is learning to live with it. If some things are abominable to you, the relationship is unlikely to last.

➢ There will be some things about you that annoy or irritate your partner. If it's within your power or desire, try to change them. If not, hope that he/she accepts them.

Marriage

All the principles of relationships apply to marriage.

The most important relationship in your life is likely to be your marriage (or long-term committed relationship). In the movie, *When Harry met Sally* (1989, dir. Rob Reiner), she says:

'When you realise that you want to spend the rest of your life with somebody, you want the rest of your life to start as soon as possible.'

Marriages start with great hope. Like bringing up children, no-one is prepared for what marriage brings. If you are lucky you will be 'happy' with the normal ups and downs that every relationship has, but you will maintain your respect and admiration for each other. If you are unlucky, you will discover in time that you don't have the same aspirations, that you grow apart, that your interests differ, that you disagree on how to bring up children, that your financial situation isn't what you anticipated and that you are basically unhappy.

Roni and I have had a very good relationship. Like nearly all marriages, we've had differences and difficulties at times. We worked on them and after 47 years we have a solid, loving relationship. We focused on the positives, particularly our shared values, the admiration we had for each other as individuals, the laughter we share and the physical intimacy that comes with love.

At our 25th anniversary function I concluded my speech as follows:

'Bottom line, 18 September 1973 to 18 September 1998, the most important question of all, have we grown into two independent pillars of strengths which support the temple of our marriage? I walked with my father to my wedding from my flat which was four blocks from the Berea Shul. Have the expectations of that buoyant young tuxedoed groom, singing all the way down the street, filling his being with the intoxicating fragrance of jasmine, been fulfilled? What about the beautiful and excited bride, actualising her mother's life-long ambition? Is the marriage the nirvana she'd hoped for? Or are all expectations doomed to be washed up on the shores of disappointment? Roni is a businesswoman. I would have her in my boardroom anytime. But has our bedroom become a "bored room"? Can we stand back at a distance, in the spaces of our togetherness, and think to ourselves, with sincerity and love, "I admire you, I still enjoy going to bed with you. I still want to be married to you?"

'Roni and I are as close now as we have ever been. It's the snugness of a crackling fire in the lounge on a snowy winter's night. It's a timeless breeze blowing on your face and through your hair on a scorching day. It's the comfort of the soft old pair of slippers that you wouldn't change for some new fashionable unwearable model. It's laughing at your favourite jokes over and over again. It's heaving a sigh of resignation and acceptance when we metaphorically squeeze the toothpaste from the middle of the tube. It's driving up the driveway of your house and articulating, "Oh boy, Home." After 25 years, can you ever get tired of listening to Beethoven or Mozart or the Cliff Adams Singers? [The Cliff Adams Singers' main fare was easy listening music including the forties, fifties and sixties.] Of course not.'

When a fly tries to settle on your fish and chips, you swat it away. It keeps the meal intact. When a minor irritation appears in a marriage, do the same. Most trivial arguments, not only in marriage, can be solved quickly when the parties realise that they are not big things in life. Marriages (and all relationships) can withstand differences – even major ones. It takes patience and understanding.

Marriage (similar principles apply to all relationships, but marriage is unique) is extremely complex. Don't get married for the wrong reason, like, 'It's time I got married', or as a response to pressure from parents or friends or someone you've been going out with for a while. The right reason is a feeling of unconditional love, admiration, respect and no desire to control the other person. It is almost a feeling of certainty that this is the person with whom you want to spend the rest of your life.

If you're uncertain, wait. Don't rush into marriage. There are fairy stories about how people get engaged after two weeks, but these are the exceptions. Get to know someone very well first.

The most important aspect of any marriage or relationship is how you talk to the other person. Don't use guilt and blame – if your partner burnt the meat on the barbeque the last thing he/she needs is, 'Didn't you see that you left it too long? How stupid of you.' Better would be,

'Oh gosh, let's see what else we've got to eat.' Be aware of your speech and how it affects your partner. As mentioned earlier, tone of voice is critical.

Practise your 'With pleasures.' This applies to all relationships. Somebody asks you to do something. If you are going to do it, just say, 'With pleasure'. Don't use a whining or bickering tone. That's like running hard chalk over a blackboard. 'Can't you see I'm reading my newspaper? You always ask at difficult times. OK, then, I'll do it and harrumph.' That just makes everyone feel bad.

You're entitled to say no. If you don't want to do it, say in a soft voice, 'Sorry, I can't do it at this time, I'm reading my newspaper.'

Listen to what your partner is saying and acknowledge his/her feelings. Every now and again you might say how lovely they look or how you admire them for doing something.

The secret of a good marriage is to leave three or four things a day unsaid. These are nagging criticisms or finding fault, however small. An example: 'You didn't fill the kettle with water after you made the tea. It's not right.' You fill it every time. This was once in a year or so. He could just say nothing. 'I can't believe that you didn't fill up the car. It was down to one bar. I could have run out of petrol.' What's the point? Just fill up the car and say nothing. The list is endless.

Have no expectations or demands of your partner – you are responsible for yourself. Don't try to control your partner. Do try to please your partner, but don't do anything that is abhorrent to you.

In company, if your partner is asked a question, don't answer for him or her. Try not to contradict your partner in public. Never humiliate your partner.

Keep your disagreements private.

Get out of an abusive relationship – the sooner the better. If your marriage is in trouble, seek counselling. Keep working at your marriage. Marriages can survive earthquakes. If it continues to be unbearable, though, for whatever reason, it may be time to end it.

Both partners should initiate sex at various times. It shouldn't always be up to one partner. If the sexual side of marriage isn't working out, seek counselling. If you don't enjoy sex and avoid it, there is a strong possibility that your partner will find it elsewhere. With respect between you and your partner, sex can continue into advanced age.

Believe in your partner.

In 1985 Roni had the possibility of buying into a training franchise from a UK company. The cost was R250,000 (around $130,000, £80,000). I didn't have the money and we agreed to abandon the idea. About a week later, unbeknown to Roni, I decided that this was possibly a great opportunity that shouldn't be missed. I went to the bank and arranged to borrow the money on the security of my New Bernica shares.

We went to dinner at the swish new Japanese restaurant at the Carlton Hotel. At an appropriate moment I gave her an envelope which contained two things – the cheque for R250,000 and a note that said, 'I believe in you.' She needed a few tissues.

The story has a much happier ending. Before the deal was consummated the UK franchisor was pressurised into getting out of South Africa by the anti-Apartheid sentiment. They gave the company to Roni at no cost and suggested that she print her own materials, still using their methodology. Roni eventually sold that company to a public company, of which she became a director.

When we moved to London in 1989 Roni joined the UK company as a senior trainer.

She says that my faith in her made her feel empowered and emboldened, ready to take on the world.

Breaking Up

'It's better to sit all night than go to bed with a dragon.'

Zen proverb

If someone you really care about breaks up with you, it's fine to feel terrible and you need to feel terrible as long as it takes before you overcome it. Hopefully you won't be a Miss Havisham.

The best thing to do is to immerse yourself in work or a hobby or physical exercise. The more involved you become, the faster you can get over your hurt. I was nearly always the person who was 'dumped' with two notable exceptions. As I was young, work and sports always distracted me and it didn't take long for me to find new girls to take out.

If you are in a 'steady' relationship and yet for some reason you sleep with someone else, no matter how guilty you feel, never tell your partner. It will be too hurtful. The confession may make *you* feel better, but unless you want to end the relationship, keep your guilt to yourself.

I had a work colleague who had a happy marriage. After a rather boozy staff party he had a dalliance with one of the secretaries. He was consumed by guilt and after keeping it in for two years he finally confessed. He explained that it was only a one-night stand (which it was) and that he wanted to apologise. His wife threw him out.

If your partner has an affair and you discover it, you have a decision to make. You will feel betrayed. You will feel angry and sad. You will want to throw things at them. You will want to walk out or want to throw them out. This is the time to recognise your feelings and to let them be known in any way you like. But, in time, it's up to you to decide what to do.

After your initial outpouring, find a quiet moment and make your plan. Write down all the ramifications of ending the relationship or staying together. It is certainly one of the most complicated situations one can ever be in. But ultimately there are only the two possibilities. Stay or split up. However distraught you may be, at some point you have to try to make the most of your life.

Relationships survive affairs and other major upheavals. It can take time to rebuild trust. If you decide to stay together, try to avoid harking back to the affair and avoid recriminations. They are not conducive to a harmonious relationship. Look forward.

If you break up with someone, they may not feel good about themselves, but they will get over it. It has to be done. If someone asks, 'What's wrong with me?' you may explain that you can't like every man or woman and you simply don't want to take the relationship further – together with most others, you don't like them in that way. It's not about them, it's about compatibility. I suggest that you never ask, 'What's wrong with me?' Just look for someone else.

If you feel you have to break off a relationship, do it kindly, but firmly. Don't go back on your decision if the other person begs and pleads and you feel sorry for them. It will only prolong the agony until next time.

In 1982, I was at a health spa in Cape Town and got talking to the masseuse. It transpired that she had been engaged for four years but was extremely unhappy and didn't know how to break off the engagement. She had four dogs that were important to her. She also had no savings and needed a job to pay her bills every month.

I very seldom give advice, but I decided to make an exception. I said that she should call a farmer friend of hers and start with the words, 'I need your help.' He would respond to that and she should ask him to take her dogs. I also said that she should call her friend in Sea Point and tell her that she may need a place to stay for a few days. The owner of a hotel in Durban was at the spa. He had told her that if she ever left that spa she would have a job at his hotel. I told her to call the hotel owner and tell him that she was taking up his offer. She must then decide on a day that she would break off the engagement.

I told her to steel herself and when her fiancé came home she should say to him, 'This relationship isn't working for me and I need to end it.' I told her not to use the word 'you' if possible, such as 'You always drink too much. You haven't got any long-term prospects, etc.' I warned her that he would beg, plead, threaten, try to intimidate her and tell her that nobody would ever love her as much as he did. I said that he would promise to change and would want another chance. I said that it was possible that he may even get physical and that she may need to go to her friend in Sea Point. I told her that she must be steadfast and not waver, even if she felt herself weakening. She must repeat that the relationship wasn't working for her and that she was certain that that wouldn't change. I gave her R300 (around $360, £200, in those days), which was the airfare from Cape Town to Durban. I then left the spa.

Six months later she called me. She got my number from a friend who saw her at her new job at the hotel in Durban. She said that she called to thank me for saving her life. She had called the farmer who was very sympathetic and took the dogs. The Durban hotel owner had responded enthusiastically.

On the night, everything happened exactly as I had said. He begged, pleaded, got angry, promised to change and said that nobody would love her more than he would! She never used the word 'you' in a derogatory manner. She said that she felt herself weakening but remembered to stick to the line and after about an hour he accepted it. They had a house together and they agreed to sell it, pay off the bond and share the proceeds. She also said that she could never have done it without the R300.

Unwanted Pregnancy

Girls: It's usually not a good idea to get pregnant unless you are in a long-term, committed relationship, preferably marriage. Take precautions! Precautions also help to avoid sexually transmitted infections.

Boys: It's usually not a good idea to make a girl pregnant unless you are in a long-term, committed relationship, preferably marriage. Take precautions!

If it does happen:

- ➢ Discuss what's happened with your parents, and/or a doctor or sympathetic friend. Don't be swayed by what other people may say or think, especially ministers of religion. They have their own agendas.
- ➢ We all have opinions on abortion. These may or may not change

when faced with the dilemma in our own life. Keep an open mind. Anything is possible. Think about the right solution for you.

➤ Boys, the decision to terminate or not is not yours, but you may be required to provide some sort of support for the child. This may concentrate your mind to be very careful, but accidents happen. Be sure you respect the girl, but you may not be able to meet all her demands.

➤ You may need legal advice.

Relationships in the Age of Smart Phones and Social Media

When I grew up, there were no cell phones or social media. In South Africa there was not even television until I was 32, in 1976. Our days were spent playing sport and board games like Monopoly, Cluedo, Wembley and Careers. There were no computer screens and we read books and went to the movies. There wasn't even direct dialling between Johannesburg and Cape Town. If I wanted to speak to my parents from my holiday in Cape Town, I had to book what was known as a 'trunk call'. It is very difficult for anybody born after 1980 to imagine the almost total lack of electronic communication that existed then.

Young people today are obsessed with cell phones and social media. Wherever you look, people are on their phones texting or on Instagram or on Facebook or TikTok or some other new app. It is such a commonplace part of life that you probably don't even realise how prevalent it is.

A few years ago, Roni and I were having dinner with friends and their teenage children, 17 and 19 years old. They are close friends and we had known the children from birth. Their phones would beep intermittently through dinner and they would text away, oblivious to the conversation. No amount of cajoling or instruction from their parents would stop the flow. 'It's just from Graeme, I have to answer it.' Graeme was the boyfriend – who can argue with that? I felt ignored by them. Not that it affected me, but it was rude, and dismissive.

In contrast we had dinner with another friend and her son. His phone rang and he immediately answered and said, 'Sorry I can't talk now. I'm with friends.' He apologised to us and switched off his phone. I wanted to spend more time with him. His undivided attention was affirming to me as a person.

If you're on a date, turn off your cell phone and focus on your partner. Anything else is rude and doesn't make the person feel good about himself/herself.

Online Dating

When we were growing up, you met people at school or university, at 'socials' (dance parties organised by synagogue or church, etc.), you were introduced by friends or at parties. Today the ability to meet new people has increased more than a thousand-fold. The internet has brought connectivity to millions of people. We tended to date people who were connected to us somehow, from a similar socio-economic background, usually from the same religion and with a similar education.

I have been married for 47 years but I wonder what I *would* do now if I were just setting out on my 'dating' life? I can see the dangers of online dating and connecting with strangers. The dangers are well documented as are the caveats like the first meeting being in a public space and not going to someone's home until you've known them for a while, etc.

I imagine that all the 'rules' that apply to every relationship should apply to someone you meet on the internet. All I would say is that because there are a great number of desperate people out there, if ever you are asked for money, run as fast as you can, even if you think you are totally in love. In fact, *especially* if you think that you are totally in love. You can be absolutely certain that if you are asked for money, everything up to that point has been a charade by the other person. Often the request will be accompanied by some terribly sad story about illness or a major world event like a flood or earthquake or the need for education or some other spurious reason. Don't fall for it. Never, ever give money to anyone you've met on the internet unless you are married to them – and perhaps not always then!

Chapter 3

Sex

This is a massive topic all on its own. It's part of the complex web of relationships (see Chapter 2), but it's important enough to merit its own chapter. I would suggest that you read books on sex and relationships, if you haven't done so already or find your own sources of information. These are a few of my subjective views, based on my experiences and observations. I had a great many anxieties and conflicts and it took me many years to reach sexual maturity. Even now there is a great deal outside of my understanding.

> ➤ Sex is fun. It's exciting, it's daring, it may be naughty, it's interesting; it's probably the most important aspect of life for most of your life.
> ➤ Sex is all about feeling good about yourself and making the person you are with feel good about themselves.
> ➤ Sex can be far more than just physical. It can be highly emotional and, at the highest level, spiritual. When there is total, unconditional love, sex completes the joining together of two souls. It is the highest form of communication and expression of love that there is.
> ➤ Making love is very much more than just sex. The two may be mutually exclusive, i.e., you can have sex without feeling love.

- Sex involves experimentation and is ultimately an acceptance of yourself as a sexual being.
- Sex is an abandonment of your inhibitions and making yourself vulnerable.

For me, sex was problematic in my formative years. If you're lucky, sex will come easily to you, whether you have one partner for life, a few or many. I was slightly less lucky, and had to work on overcoming inhibitions and fears, but I knew it was important that I did this work.

My own sexual journey was somewhat fraught and I share some of it here with so that you, as readers, will know that you are not alone if you have felt awkward or anxious around sex.

At about 13, I started doing what nearly all 13-year-old boys do. But I then fell under the spell of our local rabbi and became quite religious. Despite the strong desire, I resisted temptation for the next three years. Clearly, I had to have some release and nature would take its course in my sleep. In hindsight, this religious phase was unnatural and detrimental to my development and to my maturity.

At the end of my matriculation year in 1960, when I was 16, I had something of an epiphany and decided to end my strict religious observance. I was still overweight at close to 125kg. There was a girl at our synagogue that I rather liked, but she was almost as prudish as I was shy. Nothing was ever going to happen there.

Apart from the genetic aspect, part of the reason for the obesity was that when I was 15, I broke my ankle. I had two steel pins put into the ankle and a plaster cast from my foot to above my knee for almost six months. I had to use crutches. When that plaster cast came off I had to have a walking plaster for three months. This meant that I played no sports and was quite sedentary.

When I got to university, I started playing sports – cricket, soccer and squash. I was quite good at sport. I also started going to the gym and running in the early morning. The weight started to fall off and I became more aware of girls as they became more aware of me. I took out one or two, but there was certainly nothing too physical going on.

The slimmed-down version of me, while not in the hunk class, was mildly attractive to the more serious type of girl.

One night in 1962 (I was 18) I was fixed up on a blind date with a very precocious and mature 16-year-old girl named Judy. It was a good friend's 21st birthday and she danced very close to me. This had never happened to me before. When I dropped her at home she kissed me like I'd never been kissed. The logistics in those days were difficult. We all lived with our parents and so a lot of 'necking' took place in the car. Parental attitudes were also quite conservative. It would have been unheard of to take a girl into your room while your parents were at home. I'm sure that other boys and girls made arrangements to get around this obstacle, but I was a little naïve.

I also started dating more regularly, but I never had a serious, exclusive girlfriend. I became a little more adventurous, and two friends of mine and I rented a one-room apartment in a block of flats near our home. We did it up night-club style and we used to take girls there. However, while we did all experiment, we stopped short of intercourse – or at least I did. It was just before the Pill became popular.

One night (I was 21) after a party, I took a girl I liked very much to the apartment. With dim lighting, we played the slow, sexy music of the time – Frank Sinatra, Ella Fitzgerald, Matt Monroe, and Marianne

Faithfull. Things were going particularly well and we took off all our clothes. I'm not sure if it would have gone all the way, but, horror of horrors, suddenly not everything was in full working order.

The girl was very kind and sympathetic, and she understood my embarrassment and anxiety. 'It's not a problem,' she said. 'It's very common. Just relax, Let's lie here together and hold each other.' I think that it was quite a difficult experience for her as well, but she seemed to be knowledgeable in such matters. She remained calm and that helped me because I felt quite desperate and could have reacted unpredictably.

'Don't worry,' she said, 'Nobody will ever know about this.' I was quite relieved that she didn't ridicule me, but it was devastating for a fairly insecure, young adult (it is scary for anybody). You can imagine her empathy. After a few minutes I said that we should get dressed and I took her home.

The encounter set me back for many months. I had nobody to speak to – certainly not my parents, and I was too ashamed to speak to my friends. I had to get on with life. Fortunately, I had work, university, sports and interests, even though for the first few days and weeks it was difficult to concentrate. An event like that can have lasting damage, if not addressed. I was fortunate that I had read a poem by D.H. Lawrence which included, 'When desire has failed, all you can do is wait.'

I didn't take out any girls for a few weeks and when I did, I avoided going too far. One girl took that as a sign of indifference towards her. She wasn't used to that. She was quite forward and took the initiative to invite me to her apartment. I think that she had to prove to herself that she was desirable. Although quite fearful, I went. Fortunately all was well and I got back on the dating scene. Could my 'redemption' have been somebody else's need for acceptance?

My first consummated experience was in London in 1966 when I was almost 22 years old. It was with a girl I met at a dance at the Overseas Visitors' Club in Earl's Court. She was very extraverted and invited me back to her place. I think that I was probably the last of my friends to lose my virginity. I don't feel so bad about it, though. I recently watched the series on the life of Hugh Hefner, founder of *Playboy Magazine* and probably one of the most promiscuous men since Casanova. He said that the first time he had sex was when he was 22 and it was with his wife on their wedding night. His wife said that in those days they 'did a lot of things, but not that one thing'.

My view is that irrespective of what parents, grandparents, friends, ministers of religion, teachers or the experts may say, virginity is not a virtue. Neither is promiscuity. Virtues are things like kindness, compassion, respect and patience. However, if you want to remain a virgin until you are in a committed relationship, it is up to you.

After that initiation, I had a number of casual girlfriends and quite a few sexual experiences. However, having been overweight and having had a slow sexual development, I was never very confident and had to overcome many fears and insecurities every time I met a new girl. Of course, as time went by and I had more successes, it changed.

I was very fortunate with regard to Roni. She was very comfortable with sex. She was adventurous and liberated and enjoyed sex. She made me feel good about myself, which is the most important thing of all.

I was very vulnerable until I realised that the girls were often equally vulnerable. I made it my objective to make the girl feel good about herself. I **never, ever** said or did anything that could be hurtful about the girl's body shape or size, performance or feelings about sex. Most particularly I think it's important never to deride the size of a man's penis or the size of a woman's breasts.

Men are extremely sensitive about this and there are endless jokes and innuendoes about penis size. Some men think it really matters, but in reality, I believe that if you can get an erection, then almost any size is satisfying for a woman. Unless there is a physical deformity, your penis is normal. Focus on making your partner feel wonderful and telling them how wonderful they make you feel, thus creating a virtuous circle.

A friend of mine, whom I'll call Billy, and I were on holiday in Durban in December 1966. He was quite diffident, but had a good sense of humour and was very clever. We met a girl on the beach and Billy asked her out that night. I had my own arrangements and when I got back to our room I found Billy frantically pacing up and down.

'What happened?' I asked.

He said, 'I have never felt so terrible in my life. I've just had the most deflating insult anyone could have.'

'What was it?' I asked

He said, 'We were getting on very well, kissing and stuff, and she took off my trousers and underpants. When I was naked she said, "Hmm, I've seen bigger."'

I tried to console him and point out that the remark reflected more on her than on him and that she was coarse, insensitive and clearly ignorant. I said that I understood how upset he was and that he should stay upset until he got over it. I assured him that he would.

For the last two days of the holiday he was distracted, could hardly concentrate on our squash games and was not very communicative. He was really rattled.

We got back to Johannesburg and shortly thereafter I left for London. I lost touch with him but about 10 years after the incident I met him at a party. He was with a lovely woman whom he introduced as his wife. They had four children and were clearly still very much in love.

When I was in London in 1967, still relatively inexperienced, I went to bed with one of the bunny girls at the Playboy Club. Afterwards we were lying naked on the bed and she was looking at my body. It was shortly after Billy's experience in Durban and I wondered whether she was comparing me to any of her other numerous boyfriends.

I thought to myself, 'This is me. I can't change myself. You either like me as I am or not.' After a few moments she lay next to me and whispered, 'That was great. Some of the boyfriends I've had are so rough and only interested in themselves. But you make me feel so good about myself.' Needless to say it was a defining moment and I felt very good about *myself*! It gave me great confidence for future encounters.

What was interesting is that her one breast was quite a bit smaller than the other (or larger, depending how you look at it). It came out later that she was self-conscious about this and felt insecure, despite being attractive and popular. I did notice it, but I thought that it was irrelevant. Months later she told me that I was the only man that she had been intimate with who never commented on it. She took that as being sensitive and understanding.

Women are also sensitive about their breasts, but the reality is that most men really don't care. What they care about is how a woman makes them feel. If you feel that your breasts are too small or too big, you can have them enhanced or reduced, but in most cases, it is probably unnecessary. Focus on making your partner feel wonderful and telling them how wonderful they make you feel.

A kind word regarding a person's sexuality, body or technique can instil great confidence and can have far-reaching, positive consequences, particularly with maturing adults. 'I love the way you make love' is like jet fuel. An unkind or dismissive word can cause damage to a vulnerable person. It's like a drop of black ink in a glass of champagne.

In her ground-breaking analysis of male/female relationships in *'What the Hell is he Thinking'* (Penguin Random House, 2010) gender and dating historian Zoe Strimpel interviews hundreds of men about their experiences. One of the men says that he has performance anxiety not only when having sex with a woman for the first time, but every time. This is a hugely complex issue to which these few words cannot do justice. However, I would like to point out to the girls that a man's dignity and self-esteem may well be in your hands.

It also happens to women, just in a different way. However, you should know that this is perfectly normal and not something to fret about. The great South African cricketer, Barry Richards, said that every time he went in to bat he was nervous. As soon as the game started, there was only the moment. I'm anxious before every speech I make. After the first sentence, I'm in the flow.

Get into the habit of complimenting your partner every now and again – neither too often nor too seldom – intermittent reinforcement.

If you think that you may have an STI, do not panic. Nearly all STIs are eminently curable in a short time. Immediately go to a doctor or laboratory and get yourself tested. If you find that you are positive, contact all your sexual partners immediately.

A number of people get a clean bill of health before entering a new sexual relationship and ask their partners to do the same. This can give you quite significant peace of mind, even if it is not that romantic to start with.

Boys: never, ever try to force a girl into sex or to do anything she doesn't want to. No is really no and the most important thing in any relationship is respect for the other person. You would want your sensitivities respected, so remember that she does too.

When you are dating, or even in longer term relationships, if someone is very persistent and tries to insist that you do something you don't want to do, be very firm. If that person tries emotional blackmail, saying things like, 'If you loved me, you would do this,' you could respond with: 'If you loved *me*, you wouldn't persist with asking me to do something that I really don't want to do.' Another simple answer is, 'I obviously don't love you enough, so perhaps you should find someone who does.' It's about retaining your self-respect and dignity.

'If you loved me you would …' is actually controlling behaviour and is usually self-centred. Put yourself in the shoes of the person making this statement. 'If you loved me you would send me naked pictures of yourself.' The person is not interested in you at all. He or she wants their own self-gratification. On the other hand, 'If you loved me, you would bring me flowers every now and again' says that the person is feeling somewhat neglected. Even so, a much better way of asking may be, 'I really appreciate it when you bring me flowers.'

In general, a better way of asking for something could be, 'I would like it if you would … but I understand if it's something you really don't want to do.' You are expressing your feelings and desires but showing understanding about the other person's sensitivities. If someone is habitually controlling with little thought for you, you may need to reassess the relationship.

Never tolerate bullying of any sort. It can only lead to problems later on in the relationship, and the longer a relationship goes on, the more difficult it may be to break it off. As soon as you realise that you don't want the relationship to progress to marriage (or committed long-term relationship), after being in the relationship for a while, break it off. According to renowned US diplomat Henry Kissinger:

'A crisis not faced today will lead to far more serious consequences tomorrow.'

It's a bad idea to stay in an abusive relationship. Get out as soon as you can. Avoid people who find fault with you on a regular basis, for whatever reason. However, if what they say is valid, look at your habits and decide whether you need to change them. People can change habits and still be themselves. The same applies to you – beware of finding fault with your partner. They won't feel good about themselves.

Keep your sexual experiences private and never say anything disparaging about anybody to your friends. This confidentiality is vital. Bear in mind that if you discuss private details about someone, the person you are talking to should believe that you will discuss their private stuff with others and you will never be trusted. Furthermore, you can do the person you are speaking about some harm. Of course, we all talk about our relationships to our friends and this is natural. Just be careful not to diminish the person you are talking about.

Sex is not a silent operation. Tell your partner what you like. Especially early on, they may need some coaching as to your needs. Saying things like, 'I love it when you…' 'The way you do that makes me feel …' 'When we're in bed, I enjoy …' These affirmations make the other person feel good about themselves. Sometimes you may not like what your partner is doing and then you can say in a gentle voice, 'That doesn't feel quite right for me' or something similar. Ask questions about what your partner may like and, unless something is totally abhorrent to you, try to please them.

If at first sex is not great, don't give up immediately, especially if you like the other person. It will probably get better. It's like driving a car. In the beginning you are tentative. If you feel your partner isn't responsive to you sexually but they like you, it may be worthwhile to keep trying, but never be aggressive.

There's no need to be apologetic about your lack of experience or boast about all your conquests. Just get on with it. You never have to feel guilty or ashamed about anything you do with regard to sex. Nearly everything is 'normal' and whether you have a strong libido or a mild libido, it's fine. There are perversions and deviations that may fall outside of 'normal', e.g. paedophilia or extreme sado-masochist practices.

If you encounter a paedophile, report him or her immediately to the police or other authority.

If you want sex or masturbate seven times a week, or more, or once a month, or less, you're 'normal'. Don't listen to people who boast or show off. They're just talking about themselves and usually people who need to do this, particularly ostentatiously, are actually quite insecure. A secure person has no need to tell the world how great they are.

Distinguish between 'I love you', 'I want to go to bed with you' and 'I want to marry you'. When all three come together, that person may be the ONE. Usually 'I want to go to bed with you' comes first. In the heat of the moment, it's very easy to confuse love with sex.

If for any reason you still don't enjoy sex with someone, even after persevering for a while, but you like them in every other way, break up the relationship. Stay friends.

If something is very important to your partner (not only with regard to sex) and you don't particularly want to do it, you may want to try, in order to please your partner, but you do *not have* to if it is abominable to you.

Just because you've been to bed with someone doesn't mean they own you – and vice versa.

It may be that you go to bed with someone and you regret it later. This happens more often than you might think. Accept that it has happened; you can't undo it. With time, the regret will go away. You don't have to justify anything to your friends or acquaintances.

I recall reading about a young man who ventured out of his insulated environment and went to the big city. When he got back his friends asked him if he had met a lot of women. When he answered in the affirmative they said, 'How were you for them?' 'Fantastic for some, terrible for others,' he replied. I identified.

Pornography

Pornography is ubiquitous. It is free and can be accessed very easily. There must be a reason why it is viewed so prolifically. It is obviously titillating and everybody is interested in sex.

However, there is nothing 'loving' about pornography, whereas sex with someone you love is the ultimate expression of deep and lasting affection. Pornography is one-dimensional: there is no spirit, no heart, no feeling. It's as barren as a desert.

Pornography bears no resemblance to 'normal', everyday lovemaking experienced by the majority of people. Very few people have the bodies of the porn stars and nobody can live up to the expectation of perfect sexual performance. It's just not real life. Furthermore, a great deal of pornography, particularly regarding male genitalia, is fake, using Photoshop or similar techniques.

Pornography can give the viewer the impression that that is how sex should be. It can create anxiety in the viewer that he or she could not have the same capability or body. It can also create an expectation of another person and when they don't live up to it, there can be disappointment.

When you do have sex, appreciate each other's bodies as they are and don't compare yourself or a partner to a porn star.

If you do watch pornography, my suggestion is that you don't take it seriously. Understand why you are watching it, but dismiss any notion that it is how your sex life should be. If you find that you are watching incessantly, you need to take stock of what's happening. You may need help. Pornography can never take the place of meaningful human interaction.

Bear in mind that if you watch pornography your computer or device may end up with a nasty virus. Make sure that you have proper protection.

Chapter 4

How to Handle ... Stuff

Anger

My strong belief that you are responsible for yourself made me think at one point that all anger is really just anger with yourself. After all, you have a choice of how to react. However, I have realised that sometimes anger is brought on by a sudden circumstance and you don't have time to think about it. What *can* be in your control though is how long you allow the anger to last. Miss Havisham.

Anger can be very useful, in that it can keep you safe from an unwanted advance or an attempt to coerce you into a course of action. In these instances it is best to use your temper and not lose your temper. An expression of anger can stop the other person in their tracks. Not showing anger may encourage them to continue with the coercive or controlling behaviour.

I seldom get angry and have a large degree of patience. This comes from years of conditioning myself and also the realisation that everything that someone says is more a reflection of them than of me. It may also have something to do with the fact that I am somewhat fearful that anger could start a conflict. I am not very good at confrontations. There are times that I speak in a loud voice in order not to be taken advantage of. I always try to focus on the subject matter and not attack the person. For instance, 'It is unacceptable for you to denigrate me in that manner' as opposed to 'You are nothing short of being a pig'. It's the behaviour that is the focus, not the person.

One of my favourite jokes is, 'I am a man of infinite patience, but sometimes, as I tell Roni, even infinity has its limits.' Behind her benign smile I can see the rolling of her eyes and the gritting of her teeth. But she's such a good wife, nobody would ever know.

Too much anger can be detrimental to yourself and others. It is very difficult to live with or be friendly with someone who gets angry at the slightest minor frustration or provocation. Avoid angry people no matter how rich or attractive they appear. I can say that none of my good friends get angry very often – even with their partners. Short-temperedness is one of the greatest turn-offs.

If you are someone who gets angry quickly, read articles or books on anger and anger management and train yourself to get out of that destructive behaviour.

Apologies

'Apologising does not always mean that you're wrong and the other person is right. It just means that you value your relationship more than your ego.'

Mark Matthews

Our egos are very fragile and we often find it difficult to back down and apologise. We may see it as weakness or a loss of face, and we sometimes dig in and extend the potential conflict. It may be easier to apologise when you know that you are in the wrong or have done something that you truly regret. When the situation is not so clear, a form of apology can settle the issue and everyone can move on.

I have never had a problem with apologising. In fact my first rule of domestic conflict is 'When you're right – apologise'. The second rule is, 'When you're wrong – be contrite'. These rules may sound light-hearted, but they work. I am lucky that I am not defensive. I am quite happy to admit to any mistake and apologise. Sometimes an 'offended' person may take something you have said or done the wrong way. You could then apologise and say no malice was intended. The other person may be over-sensitive, but they are still your friend or partner and it is important to avoid resentment. People can hang on to things for years if not resolved at the time.

I once arrived home from golf half an hour after I thought I'd get home. We were having people for dinner. The drink with my golfing partners took a bit longer, the jokes and stories were flowing. I lost track of time. I was met with a tirade of how thoughtless I was, that I didn't care about anything other than my own selfish needs, that I had no understanding of the logistics and complexities of making dinner for six people and that all I thought about was golf. My initial internal reaction was that there was still plenty of time until the guests arrived, she was reacting unreasonably and that I wasn't such a bad person. I really believed that she was over-reacting and being irrational. However, it took no more than 10 seconds for me to give her a hug and apologise most profusely and to thank her for everything she does. A hug and kiss can be worth a thousand words. Peace restored.

In most cases it's better to be happy than right.

For me, the best defence mechanism is to have no defence mechanism and to just be open. People who are guarded usually do not create a positive energy. The energy remains blocked by the moat with which they are surrounding themselves. Expansive people give out positive energy which attracts most people. It's the difference between someone standing with their arms folded or opened out.

In business and politics there is a saying that one should 'never explain and never apologise'. In many cases, I think it is a good strategy for a leader to not show weakness when strong leadership is required. However, in everyday relationships with friends or partners or work mates, an apology is more likely to be a strength than a weakness. An apology can heal even the deepest of rifts.

Sometimes it helps to make an apology that isn't really an apology, such as, 'I'm sorry that you were offended. What can I do to make it better?' Politicians who don't want to admit that they are wrong use this kind of language.

There are times when you most certainly should not apologise, particularly when the other person has been malicious or hostile and wants to bully you into an apology. You need to stand your ground against bullies, unless you really know that you have erred and that you need to apologise.

Whether to apologise or not is usually a judgement call that you have to make. Benjamin Franklin said:

'Never ruin an apology with an excuse.'

Assertiveness

Being a rather diffident person growing up, I was not particularly assertive. However, with maturity, particularly in business, I became more assertive. What was important was that I needed to be well prepared. Assertiveness without information can be dangerous. Think of an egocentric leader who reacts impulsively without sufficient information. Taken to the extreme, a powerful despot could press the nuclear button. The greater the knowledge, the more certainty one has.

Whilst I always welcomed debate and different opinions, there came a time for decisiveness. I had to make the call, particularly in the business world.

In 1988 in South Africa, there was a war on the Angolan border. The government was defending its apartheid policy and holding on to its control of Namibia, which was called South West Africa. Conscription was compulsory and my cousin's son was killed on that border. David was 12 years old and about to enter high school. There was no indication at that time that things would change so dramatically in South Africa and I suggested to Roni that David should finish his education in London so that he wouldn't have to be called up to the army after school.

Roni was a director of a public company and I was running a public company. It was going to be a huge upheaval to emigrate and we would both be sacrificing our careers for something unknown. We weren't particularly political, but we were very concerned about the future in South Africa for our children. We both had aging parents in Johannesburg, which made the decision even more problematic. Roni is very strong willed and capable and we debated the move long and hard. I was very much for the move, Roni was not so sure. We could have been at a real stalemate. I decided that I had to be assertive and she accepted the move, albeit somewhat reluctantly.

Assertiveness is different from anger. Assertiveness is an expression that you are as important and your voice has as much validity as anyone else's. The opposite of being assertive is to allow yourself to be a doormat. Without a degree of assertiveness, you will be unable to get ahead and will be left to languish.

Too much assertiveness could be seen as being pushy and obnoxious. It says that you are the only one whose opinion or needs count. It is a matter of judgement as to how assertive you need to be. In an emergency you need to be extremely assertive if the situation demands it!

On the other hand, you may feel diffident and find it hard to be assertive. One of the great composers, Lorenz Hart, was so unassertive that it was said that if he was drowning, he would find it difficult to ask for help in case he inconvenienced anyone. If this is you, consider taking assertiveness training.

Forgiveness

Nobody's perfect. We all make huge mistakes. Think of the great biblical characters whom we revere. King David sent Uriah the Hittite into battle and had him murdered by proxy, ordering his troops to abandon him so that David could take Uriah's wife Bathsheba. That's an extreme example. We all say things we regret. We exclude people that we shouldn't. We're rude to or belittle someone to show how powerful we are, or we ignore someone's feelings.

Frequently, forgiveness happens when someone apologises. We have to decide whether we want to forgive them or not. That entirely depends on your view of a future relationship with that person.

I had a business partner who undermined me with other partners and who told lies about me to other advisers. I called him in and told him that the partnership was over. At first he was very defensive because he thought that he would win the battle with our other partners. When he found that the other partners backed me, he tried to apologise and made a whole lot of promises about how he would behave in future. Lawyers were involved and my lawyer thought that the promises he made sounded reasonable and suggested that I should reconsider my position. We had had a successful partnership in the past. I said, 'If he would seek forgiveness by squirming like a snake for 50 yards along a gravel path, naked, I still would not take him back.' My lawyer told his lawyer that he thought that there was no chance of any reconciliation! My lawyer was quite taken aback at my aggressive language. I had to make my point most forcefully.

On the other hand, I once had a huge row with Roni. Unprovoked, she said something extremely hurtful when I made a suggestion about what we should do one evening. I wouldn't like to say exactly what she said but I was shattered. I stormed out of the room and didn't want to talk to her. We were on holiday at a resort in Portugal and I didn't return to our room for three hours. She tried to call me on my phone but I wouldn't answer. When I got back to the room, she apologised most profusely. I knew that we had a long future ahead. I also knew that I wasn't going to hang on to this for 30 years, like Miss Havisham. I knew that I had to forgive her at some point, so why not now? A hug sorted it all out. I have not mentioned it again because there would be no point. I have no hard feelings about the incident, even though I haven't forgotten it. It was a rare case. There have been many other times where I needed her forgiveness.

In long-term personal and business relationships we forgive each other quite often. However, if there are too many times when forgiveness is required it may be best to end the relationship.

I started the book talking about big things in life. Forgiveness recognises that there are very few really big things in life that can't be sorted out with an apology and forgiveness.

Most things are seven-day wonders. Very few things are so big that forgiveness is not appropriate and desirable.

- ➤ In every relationship there will be times when the other person offends or upsets you in some way. Without forgiveness there would very soon be no relationships.
- ➤ Try to understand why the person did or said something. Perhaps what they did wasn't intended to offend and be sure that your feelings are not misplaced.
- ➤ The longer you hold on to a grievance, the greater the negative effect on you.
- ➤ Forgiveness allows you to move on and develop the relationship.
- ➤ Forgiveness can bring you closer to the person you are 'forgiving'.
- ➤ Forgiveness shows great maturity. Young children sometimes don't know how to forgive immediately and it may take them time.
- ➤ By being responsible for yourself, you can choose how to handle the actions or words of the person who has offended you.

➤ If you make a dreadful mistake, you would want forgiveness, so be generous in giving it.

Good Manners

'Good manners are ageless, priceless and classless.'
Diana Mather, etiquette and media coach

Good manners are attractive and even sexy. Boorish behaviour, such as pushing and shoving, swearing indiscriminately and speaking in a loud voice is a major turn-off. We were brought up always to stand up when a woman came into the room, always to say please and thank you and always to let a woman go first out of a lift or through a door. In a bus or train, we always stood up for women or elderly people. It showed respect and consideration. Even today, whenever I let a woman go first it is usually greeted with an almost surprised comment about 'how nice it is to see old-fashioned good manners'. We would also open the car door for our dates, which was always met with a smile of appreciation. It does wonders for the ego. I don't see this happening much these days. As a grandfather I so appreciate it when my grandchildren are polite and respectful.

I cannot emphasise enough the importance of 'thank you.' I make it a point of thanking everyone who does anything for me. When I receive an email or message I say, 'Thanks for the note.' It goes without saying that I express appreciation to all service providers, from the garage attendant who fills my car to my City lawyers. At home, it's just as important. 'Thanks for dinner. Thanks for tidying up. Thanks for taking out the garbage. Thank you for those kind words. Thanks for dealing with the bank.' It's all part of making people feel good about themselves.

Trust

One of the most important aspects of any relationship, business or personal, is trust, implicit or explicit. All relationships will break down unless there is complete trust of the other person.

From the time we are born, we have to trust the people around us – first our parents, then our friends, our partners, our teachers, and our children. Even when driving, we trust that the drivers of the other cars will drive carefully and stay on their side of the road. Life would be intolerable if we didn't have a fundamental trust in others. That is not to say that trust cannot be lost; it can.

In 1977 a young cricketer (23), Peter, came to play for my cricket club in Johannesburg. I got on very well with him. Roni was going overseas to visit her grandparents with David and her mother. I invited him to come and stay with me at our house for three weeks. I really didn't know him well at all. We had played a few cricket games together and he seemed like a reasonable person. I didn't consciously think of whether I trusted him or not, but in retrospect I must have trusted him implicitly. It probably worked the other way around. If I had thought that he was a bit dodgy, I wouldn't have invited him. It led me to believe that we automatically trust most people who don't display unpleasant characteristics.

When Roni returned, Peter stayed on. Soon after, Roni went to the doctor who gave her a penicillin injection. Unbeknown to anyone, Roni was allergic to penicillin and soon after her doctor's visit, she started having difficulty breathing. Peter was home and drove her straight back to the doctor who was able to give her an antidote. My inherent trust was repaid.

In his inaugural speech, John F. Kennedy said, 'Sincerity is subject to proof.' Sometimes it's not good enough to take people at their word. In fact, in business, the proof is essential and it must be committed to writing. Gone are the days when deals could be done on a handshake.

There was a time when my trust was breached, and I felt violated. I had trustees of a trust who abused their position and extracted much higher fees than they were entitled to. When I discovered it, I took legal advice. There was not much I could do because of the complex regulations and litigation would be very expensive. I fired them but had lost a lot of money.

Sometimes our trust might be an imposition on the other person. For instance, a father could say to his daughter that he 'trusts her' not to have sex before marriage. If she does so, is she betraying his imposed so-called trust? Did he have the right to make the demand and should she take on his imposition?

Sometimes, you are in a position of trust. In your work or in any organisational position it is incumbent on you to exercise total care and everybody has the right to trust you to carry out your obligations. In other words, you take on the obligation. You can also expect everybody in the organisation to fulfil *their* duties and obligations. I have noted (in the general principles) that you can have no expectations or demands of anybody. But in a workplace, a job has to be done and, in these circumstances, you are justified in expecting someone to do their job. The failure to do so could result in their losing that job.

I believe that true love is beyond trust. It is beyond the thought of trust. It is implicit. If I have to think, 'I trust you', I would already be feeling insecure. Insecurity is not love. This is a difficult concept to grasp, but it's worthwhile thinking about.

There are numerous unwritten and unspoken rules of trust, which, if broken, can lead to breakdown of relationships. For instance, if someone has an affair, it would be a breach of the 'unthought of' trust. If your friend speaks badly of you to someone else, the relationship may be fractured (temporarily or permanently). Trust will have to be rebuilt.

You can forgive a breach of trust if you want the relationship to continue, although you will probably be less inclined to trust that person in the future. If it happens again, you may need to end the relationship.

Jealousy and Envy – 'I wish I could be like you or have what you have'

Jealousy pertains to more than one party: 'I am jealous of your girlfriend.' There are three people involved – you, the person you are speaking to, and the girlfriend.
Or, 'I am jealous that our father doesn't show me as much attention as he does to you.'

Envy relates to two people: 'I am envious of your looks, your wealth, your house, your equanimity, your hobbies, your achievements, and your popularity.'

Envy is one of the most prevalent human emotions. We all feel envious sometimes. American writer Ambrose Bierce said:

'Calamities are of two kinds: Misfortune to ourselves and somebody else's good fortune.'

There is a proverb that says:

'There is something in the misfortune of even our best friends that we find not unpleasant.'

These are not welcome thoughts – and usually do not apply to major misfortunes, but they are nonetheless true.

Unless you are really insecure, you don't want to see your friends hurt in any way. But when it does happen you may feel, 'I'm happy it wasn't me.' I know that this has happened to me.

You may also briefly have a feeling of 'superiority' when a friend or acquaintance has a mishap. If you do, you may feel 'mean' or 'unworthy' for having such feelings, but don't despair. They are common to almost everyone in the world. What you need to do is recognise the feeling, accept that it is there and then let it pass through you. You will find that you really want your friends to succeed, even if you are going through a bad patch yourself. If the feeling persists, just wait – it will go away after a while.

'Jealousy and envy is the poison that kills you while not affecting the other person at all.'

When I find myself in this situation, I recognise the feeling and watch it. The result is that it lasts a shorter and shorter time. Sixty or so years ago it may have lasted a few days or weeks or even months. It's now down to a few minutes and, in most instances, a few seconds. I recognise that somebody else's success is not my failure. I'm usually genuinely pleased with my friends' successes, even if they crow about it!

When I was about 18 years old, I was extremely envious of practically everybody. I was somewhat gauche, had no girlfriends, wasn't very good at anything and thought that I was pretty much hopeless. If my teammates failed at cricket, it would make me happy. If a friend was rejected by a girl, it made me feel 'superior' because I hadn't been rejected. As I matured, I became aware of how much this was poisoning me. One Saturday evening when I was 18, I read in *The Prophet*,

'Beware the cripple who hates dancers.'

I jumped off my bed and started pacing the floor, rubbing my head. It was an epiphany. I was looking in the mirror. I was indeed the cripple.

I made a resolution there and then to not let it affect my feelings for my friends. I decided to say kind, supportive things like 'Well done on your success' or 'You must be very proud of …' When I did it, they always felt good about themselves and I'm certain that's why I have so many good friends. I didn't like being an emotional cripple.

I still have very occasional twinges of envy when people tell me how much money they have made or how wonderful their children and grandchildren are or some other source of pride for them, but I never give off the negative energy or drain the other person's energy. The envy always disappears in a couple of minutes at most. I think that if it persisted I would live with it, but I would never contaminate the atmosphere with negative comments.

I'm sure that some of my friends and acquaintances have felt envious of me at some point. It's natural. I have never let it affect me. People may be envious of me but I am not responsible for their feelings. One of my friends once asked me if I felt guilty for flying business class. I said that I don't feel guilty about anything.

I try to steer clear of envious people who bring negative energy.

Comparisons and 'What will people think?'

I've always believed that two things will destroy you if you let them: continually comparing yourself to others and worrying too much about what people will think of you.

Comparisons

There will always be someone better-looking, funnier, richer, faster, cleverer, or more self-assured than you.

For me, comparisons nearly always led to envy or a feeling of inferiority or superiority. When I had very little money, I was uncomfortable around people with a lot of money. I would find myself fawning or being diffident. I never realised that their wealth was independent of who or what I was. When I had the 'cripple who hates dancers' epiphany,

I tried to eliminate the venom of comparisons, but in reality I find that it continues even at this age. The difference is that the feeling is very transitory. It's always not the feeling that's the problem. It's how long it lasts for.

I take people for what they are. Even the rich and famous are just human and some have major flaws. Take Prince Andrew who is embroiled in a most unpleasant scandal involving sex with underage girls. He was dismissed from public duties in the UK and is disgraced. Everyone has their weaknesses, including me, and that's just part of life. I accept my shortcomings and continually try to overcome them.

There was a time when I used what could have been a negative comparison to change my behaviour positively. I mentioned Ealing Cricket Club earlier. I didn't know any of the people and wasn't sure how I would fare. There was one particular batsman who was very self-assured and was by far the best player. I admired his batting, but the comparison with my own was making me feel inferior. When I became aware of this, I thought I would look at the situation differently. I thought that instead of being envious, what I should really do was to imitate what he was doing.

I chatted to him and asked him what he thought was the secret of his success. It was quite simple – he practised more and was focussed. He also had a mental mindset that he had the bat and he wasn't going to be intimidated by any bowler, however fast. I never missed practice and that year I had my best batting average ever. My game was actually transformed. Instead of having negative thoughts about comparisons, he became my role model.

I used that strategy in later life, particularly in business. I was never afraid to ask for help or advice and instead of comparing myself to successful people I sought them out to find out why they were so good. I made them allies.

When I compared myself to people who I thought were 'inferior' it made me feel good for a while. But when I really thought about it, I decided it was very sad that my 'happiness' depended on somebody else's misfortune. That comparison was almost as damaging as my envy of successful people. There are a lot of people who get pleasure from seeing others fall. Of course I have some *schadenfreude* occasionally, as long as I don't let it last more than a few minutes.

What will people think?

Growing up I was painfully concerned with 'What will people think?' I never wanted to be mocked or laughed at because I had failed. It is most surprising that I played competitive sports like cricket – which I loved – because every time you go into bat you risk being out first ball.

I was tentative in most things that I did. When I did pluck up the courage to ask a girl out, I was hesitant in case I said something wrong. I was somewhat afraid to make a physical move because I was concerned about what she would think if I was awkward or gauche. I was scared of what she might say to her friends. The result was that I held myself back.

This also applied to my work. In my early years as the investment manager of L&G, I was afraid to put forward a slightly contradictory view because I was anxious about the board's reaction. I'm not sure exactly what the catalyst was but one day I wrote down my feelings. I wrote:

> *'They have chosen me to make the most money I can for the company. The only way I can do that is to back my judgement. I need to be very thorough with my research and preparation, but then I have to state my case clearly and with confidence and not care what they think. I am ready for different opinions, but that's why there's a market.'*

At the next board meeting, I presented a very strong case for making certain investments. One of the board members who was an extremely prominent businessman and very vocal pointed out that my views were contrary to the views of some of the biggest institutions in the country. I said that I knew that, because quite a few of the stocks we had purchased came from those institutions, particularly one. I stood my ground, despite the opposition. I'm certain that my belief in myself and not caring what anyone would think was largely responsible for the success of the company.

There is a positive side to being concerned about what people will think. It might prevent you doing something very stupid. For instance you may be tempted to steal something. The thought of what people may think of you if you were caught could prevent you from doing it.

I have also found that in most cases, nobody really cares what you do as long as it doesn't hurt anyone else. Your success or failure may be the subject of a short dinner time conversation. Your successes will be admired or envied and your failures may be sympathised with or rejoiced over. But really everybody, apart from your close friends and family, just focuses on themselves.

Possessiveness

I believe possessiveness is one of the most self-centred and selfish behaviours there is. It is an insidious form of control that forces one person in a relationship to be at the other's beck and call.

'Love possesses not nor would it be possessed: For love is sufficient unto love.'

Kahlil Gibran

For example, you enjoy playing squash after work and your partner says that they want you home earlier. You enjoy an evening out with your friends but your partner doesn't want you to go out because he or she is needy and doesn't want to be alone for a couple of hours.

I gave the example of the dancer who subjugated herself to her fiancé's possessiveness. He was narcissistic and showed great insecurity and jealousy. Why would anybody want to stop someone they love from developing their talent to the fullest of their ability? We all need fertile ground in which to grow.

A truly loving relationship will exclude possessiveness and similar controlling behaviour. Each partner will want the other to succeed in the best way possible, even if that means that the other receives accolades and admiration from many people. It may be natural to feel threatened by the overt attention of someone towards your partner. You need to have a strategy for coping with these feelings. Becoming aggressive and even more possessive might have the opposite effect of 'bringing the person into line'. Feeling confined and restricted, they may pursue an outside relationship because it gets them away from the possessiveness.

On the other hand, a light-hearted comment such as, 'I noticed that Rosemary was particularly friendly towards you. It's nice to be admired, isn't it?' may totally defuse the situation. Your partner doesn't feel restricted and you have acknowledged his or her feelings.

> *'No matter how happily married a woman may be, it always pleases her to discover that there is a nice man who wishes she were not.'*
> American satirist and writer H.L. Mencken

Roni is very successful in her career of coaching chief executives. Her work involves travelling all over the world. She has been doing this for 30 years and meets people of all ages. She is feted by literally hundreds of people every year. She receives letters of gratitude and is in constant demand. I couldn't be happier for her. I've always encouraged her. I'm happy to say that I have never felt jealous or possessive. She has no doubt been the recipient of many an advance, especially in the earlier years of her career. It has never bothered me.

She articulated that she felt blessed that I had provided fertile ground for her to grow. I feel the same about her.

Even when I was younger and quite insecure, I was lucky enough to never feel possessive about any of the girls I took out. At one level, possessiveness precludes respect for the other person.

Bullying

I was never really bullied, possibly because I didn't stick my neck out and I kept out of the way of the bullies. I was sometimes teased about my weight. It was hurtful, but somehow it didn't affect me too much and I got on with life. I was lucky enough to have very good friends who accepted me as I was. One friend called me 'Tubby' but it was good natured and I didn't take offence.

I don't have extensive experience with bullying but these are my observations. One of the most difficult experiences one can have is being bullied and teased. This is particularly difficult for school children who haven't formed any coping mechanisms, but it can extend into adulthood. Bullying is coercive behaviour and is intended to force you into doing something that the bully wants you to do. Or it may just be spiteful.

Whilst in the midst of being bullied, it is difficult to be objective. However, if you are aware in advance of what bullying is and how to handle it you may be better placed to cope.

Bullies are desperate to get their own way, irrespective of how they do it and who they hurt. Their main tools are the threat of physical violence, threat of exclusion, or threat of confiscation of property and material or financial loss. Authorities can try to bully people by using threat of incarceration or confiscation of assets.

A bully wants to exclude you or cause discomfort to you because you are a threat to them socially or your views are a threat to theirs. Taken to extremes, bullying may drive you to seek legal advice or even go to the police.

It is safest to assume that the bully will do what they're threatening. Whatever it is, prepare for it and work out how you will handle it. For instance, the person may say that unless you do something, he (or she) will tell your friends or put it on Facebook and you will never want to show your face again.

Generally, you should resist doing what the bully wants. Your real friends will stick with you and will most likely shun the bully in time.

If the bully is a person of authority, like a sports coach or teacher or boss, who may have power over you, the situation is more fraught, especially if you think that your future is dependent on them. In fact, the more the person has authority over you, the more you should resist their demands. There are countless stories of (mainly) women who have succumbed to sexual advances from bosses or people in authority. They have bitterly regretted it later. Some bullies have got their comeuppance, such as movie producer Harvey Weinstein and Fox News CEO Roger Ayles. The 'Me Too' movement has been instrumental in exposing these powerful predators, but it still happens all the time on a smaller scale.

If a coach is exhorting you to try harder and do better or you will be dropped from the team, that's not bullying. That's a coach wanting you to do better! Bullying is when the coach is actually nasty or wants you to do something inappropriate and if you don't do it, you will be demoted. Whatever the consequences might be, it is important to confront the bully upfront. Tell them that if it continues you will report it and that you want to be treated entirely on your merits. It is usually a good idea to give the bully one chance before reporting it, but definitely only one.

It takes courage to stand up to people in authority, but you need to do it. It will forever ensure that you are not a victim, subjugated to the whims of unscrupulous individuals.

However, you must be certain that the behaviour you are reporting is not frivolous or inconsequential. You shouldn't impugn someone for harmless 'banter'. Whether something is 'banter' or not is a judgement call, but you should be able to distinguish something threatening from something fairly frivolous. If the 'banter' gets serious, accompanied by physical or emotional threats, you should take action.

Try and keep a sense of humour: if someone tells a joke of a sexual nature, it is best to laugh it off and make some remark that shows that you are not offended. Prudishness may not get you very far, but if you really are offended, let the person know. Racist jokes cannot be tolerated. Even then, it may be best to express your view, in a calm voice, that you don't like the joke. It's usually not effective to be self-righteous.

You can do two things with an insult: you can either let it affect you or you can ignore it and let it be a spur for growth and independence. That takes strength of character. Remember that every statement in the universe (including this one) is a reflection of the person doing the saying and may have little to do with the subject matter. When you realise that it may be easier to know that you never have to take anything personally.

Don't lose sight of the fact that you are responsible for yourself, no matter what someone tries to do to you. You can feel injured and hurt, but you need to act in your best interests. You may deem it best to stay silent or to report the person. Either way, it is your choice – and you do have a choice.

The same particularly applies to online bullying or trolling.

A friend's grandson, aged 18, posted a picture of himself and some friends on Instagram. An anonymous posting came back saying that he was ugly and that the other friends were stupid for mixing with him. Naturally he was distressed. I recognised his feelings of humiliation and murderous intent.

'Chris,' I said, 'You are not alone in this. I'm going to ask you to theoretically make the same anonymous post.'

Chris wrote down the exact wording.

'Now Chris, how do you feel?'

'I feel nasty. I feel smug that I have brought someone down. I feel powerful that I can hurt someone. I don't like these feelings, because I feel like I'm a loser.'

'Chris, can you see that that post actually had nothing to do with you? It's all about the insecurity of the cowardly anonymous poster. If he had had any guts he would have signed the post. He only makes those posts because he is a failure. Successful or emotionally secure people always try to elevate people. He is like the ultimate cripple who can't dance. The only pleasure he gets is to cut everyone else's legs off. He is totally emotionally constipated. Is this the kind of person you want to control your feelings?'

I told him that one way to handle verbal bullying is to paraphrase a well-known sceptic who was nominated for the Nobel Prize. He said, 'If I wanted my work judged I'd go to a more competent authority.' I paraphrase that to, 'If I wanted my life judged I'd go to a more competent authority.'

'I understand what you're saying, Arnie, but it still hurts.'

'Chris, stay hurt as long as you need to. At some point you will get over it. This is a test of your character. I can give you the utmost assurance that you will come out of it, even if it doesn't seem like it at this time. Let's talk about it in a month's time.'

A week later Chris came to see me. 'Arnie, my friends all rallied around me. They said what you said, except in less polite language. They called him an asshole. I'm not going to let my self-esteem be affected by such a moron. I also remembered what you said about the competent authority. Any further trolling will be flushed down the toilet where it belongs. I certainly won't show that I'm hurt. I'm now pleased that this has happened. I feel stronger and better able to cope with negative people. I just don't have to take things personally.'

I was delighted with the outcome and even more pleased that a young man had actually listened to and acted on the 'guidance' of an old man.

Clearly you shouldn't be a troll.

Included in bullying is bitchiness or spitefulness. 'I notice that you find it difficult to put together a really smart, matching outfit. That skirt just doesn't go with the top. You need to get some taste.' Why would anybody say this? It says nothing about the outfit. It says that the person doing the saying in a spiteful voice is very insecure. He or she needs to bring you down because that's the only way that they can feel good.

The worst outcome for the bully is if they have no impact, as happened with David at his school.

Being bullied is one of the ultimate tests of your character. That's the time to dig deep and show steel. Make your plan and fight back with all the resources at your command.

Physical Fitness

Obesity ran in the Witkin family. Until I was about 17, I had a problem with my weight and it was only in my late teens that I started to get fit. I would run through the suburb in the mornings, go to the gym at lunchtimes or after work and also play sport. I played a lot of squash, which demands a certain level of fitness and I played excellent cricket and soccer. Only later in life when I became ill, did my physical fitness deteriorate, but I remain a keen golfer.

An important part of my growing up was to take control of my weight and to discipline myself to get fit. There is no doubt that the fitter I became, the better I felt about myself. I wanted to play sports at the highest level that I could reach and to do that I had to be as fit as I could be. I was never fanatical but it was enough to compete at a high level.

I combined the exercise with a healthy diet and regime. It was difficult to turn over habits of a lifetime, such as an 'addiction' to chocolate, but I realised that it was essential. I can't give any advice on diet, but for me I decided that I could eat anything I liked – just less than I usually had. Between 1961 and 1965 I went from 120 kgs (260 lbs) to 80 kgs (180 lbs). I went from the Old Parktonians 4th XI that played in the bottom league in the Transvaal to the 1st XI that played at the highest level in the Transvaal. The 4th XI came last in that league and

I was once dropped from that team. Did that make me the worst player in the Transvaal?

Physical fitness is an essential part of the eternal triangle of Love, Health and Money. All mental health professionals advocate exercise as a way to alleviate depression or similar difficulties. When I went through a bad time mentally due to the coronavirus pandemic, a therapist strongly advised me to walk and do exercises. I became active through online programmes, felt fitter and more alive which helped me out of my downward spiral of negative thoughts. Exercise was one of the keys to my rehabilitation.

Personal Hygiene

It might seem unnecessary to highlight something that should be second nature to us all. However, I'm astonished by how messy, dirty and even smelly people can be.

In households that are fortunate enough to have domestic help, young people are accustomed to having someone else 'pick up after them'; to clean the bathroom and kitchen, wash and put away their clothes, and generally keep things tidy.

When I lived in London in 1966, a number of my friends from South Africa had small bedsits or shared a flat with others. I found that most of them used to leave towels unfolded, dirty dishes in the sink, unmade beds, papers lying around and generally a mess. I shared a flat with a friend and we agreed on day one – no hairs in the bath, toilets always clean, no dirty dishes left in the sink, beds always made (even though we had our own bedrooms), and no smoking in the apartment (even though neither of us smoked).

I soon discovered that cleanliness and tidiness are sexy and that dirty or smelly people are particularly unsexy. It was fashionable in those days for young people to take gap years and travel through Europe, usually following the guidebook, 'Europe on $5 a day'. They were always looking for places to stay that wouldn't cost much. Word got around that my friend and I were receptive to helping out these travellers for a night or two.

One of the girls that came to stay with us was pleasantly aghast at the pristine state of the apartment. Her reaction was that she soon indicated in no uncertain terms that she was interested in more than just a place to stay for a couple of nights. She was quite attractive but smelt of smoke and I thought that she hadn't had a bath for a while. Of course she could have cleaned up, but at that point it was too late. I had to make an excuse that wasn't hurtful, so I said that I had a current girlfriend – which I didn't have. That made her want me even more because she thought that I was very decent. I didn't want to disillusion her.

Roni is extremely neat, tidy and clean and keeps everything in the house in perfect order. I too am impeccable when it comes to cleanliness. I think if either of us wasn't like that, it would be impossible to live together. Both of us always wipe down sticky surfaces, never leave crumbs on the floor that could attract ants, never leave the toilet dirty and always wash dishes immediately after use. We are both meticulous when it comes to our daily personal hygiene. Roni always removes her make up before bed.

In the golden triangle of health, money and love, personal hygiene is essential.

Education

'The ink of the scholar is more precious than the blood of the martyr.'
The Prophet Muhammad

I was a good student. Not brilliant, but I was conscientious, although I probably could have worked harder. I did well at school, obtaining one distinction in my matriculation year and lots of Bs. As an accountancy student at university I relaxed in the first year and just scraped through all my subjects. In my second year, I was repentant about that first year, so I put in extra effort and came second in the class. Thinking that this was all easy, I barely passed third year, getting four thirds. With that shock in mind, I worked extremely hard in my final year and once again came second in the class.

Your education is extremely important because it is there for life. I would urge you to work consistently hard and to take your exams very seriously. Your education will give you the tools to fulfil your purpose.

Be curious and hungry for information (even into old age) and enjoy the process of learning. Whenever you can, read. In these days of video games, Netflix, live streaming, television and social media it takes great discipline to take the time.

'A reader lives a thousand lives before he dies ... The man who never reads lives only one.'

George R.R. Martin

A book holds up a mirror in a way that nothing else does. Only you are looking in the mirror. If you like what you see you can moderate your behaviour. If the suit doesn't fit, don't wear it. Some of my greatest changes of behaviour have come from reading, particularly Kahlil Gibran and *Great Expectations*!

When you're studying for exams, the most important thing is to focus. Block out all social media at certain times and concentrate on your studies. When I was in Grade 8, I was quite a good student. I used to come in the top eight in the class, but never higher than fifth. There were two geniuses in our class: Anthony Ginsberg and Terence Wilson. The highest mark for the term 'marksheets' was 600. Anthony got around 590 and Terence got around 580. One particular term, I decided to be disciplined and to focus. Throughout the term there was no sport until my homework was completed correctly. When it was close to exam time, my friends were quite worried about me when I ensconced myself in my room. I forsook my usual casual approach, doing enough to get through, but not enough to get the best out of myself.

That term I came second. The teachers were astonished, but not as much as my parents and friends. I could do it if I put my mind to it. The realisation that focus was so powerful was another epiphany. Whenever I need to do something important, I recall that focus.

Higher education is not for everyone. There are a great many successful people who didn't finish school. What is important is to realise that life itself is an education. The 'University of Life' can provide you with all the information you need. You just need to apply the information. Your attitude to your profession will determine success or failure. A golf coach, or high court judge or a beautician doesn't need to know who won the Hundred Years War. However, someone passionately interested in history will need to know who won all the wars since time immemorial.

If you do enter university, give it everything you've got. It is very expensive and you owe it to your parents and yourself to do the best you can. By all means have the great fun that is almost as important as the syllabus.

If you don't go to university, your education nevertheless continues; everything that happens to you is part of your 'education.'

Skills and Hobbies

I always wish I'd developed more skills. I am hopeless at fixing things or doing anything artistic. I do know a bit about first aid. Fortunately, I've never been called on to do a Heimlich manoeuvre or revive someone who has collapsed. I suggest that you develop skills and nurture your hobbies. It takes focus and dedication, but the things you learn to do will serve you well in all aspects of your life.

When Roni and I were first married, I bought her a guitar. She had played a bit at university. After about nine months, the guitar sat forlornly in the cupboard gathering dust. I thought, 'Okay, I'll take you out of your misery.' I looked in the classified advertisements of *The Star* newspaper and found an entry, 'Guitar lessons. Call Rocky.' Rocky lived on the 30th floor of an apartment building in a suburb called Hillbrow. I called him and embarked on this adventure.

It was one of the most liberating experiences of my life. I practised every day and became quite proficient. After about six months, Rocky solemnly announced that he felt he couldn't teach me any longer. He said that my singing was so bad that he just couldn't take it. His economic exigencies weren't worth the assault on his ears. He said that if I took singing lessons, then he would continue. He put me in touch with a woman aptly named Melody.

For an hour every Saturday morning for 12 years, and once a month for another 12, I could be Frank Sinatra or Matt Monroe or Tony Bennett and float on a reverie of romance and eternal love, or the loss of eternal love. The world could be burning, but it couldn't touch me in my fantasy hour. Rocky continued to teach me guitar. I believe that I went from terrible to bad to just about acceptable. However I was good enough to sing when David's school put on a show for their 'family day'. I also sang at a number of 'soirees' that I organised.

I would strongly recommend taking up a musical instrument. It takes discipline to find time to practice, but it will give you immense pleasure for a lifetime.

One of my skills was chess. I played for my school and in the seventies, I joined the Johannesburg Chess Club. I went from the second bottom of 10 divisions to the top division in two years. The top division had five or six South African champions. I came seventh.

I 'invented' an attacking opening on move three. I played it in the Johannesburg Open in 1975. The chess correspondent of the *Star* newspaper, former South African champion Kurt Dreyer, wrote up the game against Eddie Price, also a former SA champion. He concluded that the 'Witkin Gambit' was perfectly playable. There are very few people in the world, including the iconic players, Gary Kasparov and Bobby Fischer, who have innovated on move three.

A week before the publication of this book I consulted International Grandmaster Dejan Bojkov, an expert in the Alekhine's Defence. He had never seen the move before and after a brief analysis he too concluded that it was a sound innovation on move three. In fact he said that he would like to be white especially if black accepts the sacrifice. I hope that in time it may receive more analysis.

In my retirement I can pit my wits on the internet. There is a strong revival of chess following the series 'The Queen's Gambit.' For those of you who play chess the moves are in the Alekhine's Defence:

1 E4 Nf6
2 E5 Nd5
3 F4

The pawn can be taken freely. What I gain is momentum. I have a friend in Canada who plays frequently online and whenever possible he plays the Witkin Gambit. He nearly always wins.

In the seventies my friend, Graeme Levin, and I invented two games. One was a stock exchange game called 'Speculate' and it was marketed by the games giant Waddingtons, whose games included Monopoly at the time. In that year they developed only four games of the 2,000 prospects they received.

The other game was a card cricket game which we sold through Graeme's magazine *Games and Puzzles*.

Roni and I also play bridge. We are in good company. Warren Buffett and Bill Gates play frequently on the internet. Golf has been a saviour for me. I play three times a week and enjoy it immensely. These are good pastimes in advanced age!

> ➢ Take a first aid course or read up on basic first aid. You never know when you may need to help someone.
> ➢ Art, woodwork, DIY and sports are all creative activities worth nurturing. They can be useful and they boost your self-confidence. With art or writing the experience is probably as important as the end result.
> ➢ Being useful around the house can save a lot of money and also time if workmen are difficult to get hold of.

Winning and Losing

I am very competitive, although very few people would know it. I always do my very best to win in any game I play, even with my grandchildren. I take things seriously enough to do really well, but not so seriously as to lose sight of the pure enjoyment of playing the game. My style is to compliment my opponent on a good shot or a clever play and never to use gamesmanship. I'm not playing for money, so I don't have to win at all costs. Professionals often use dodgy tactics, especially if it will be difficult for the referee to spot them. I never try to put my opponents off with snide or sarcastic remarks. In golf there is a great deal of 'chirping,' which I think is unsportsmanlike. I'm in the minority.

In cricket, at all levels from the playground to test cricket, there is a great deal of 'sledging'. This is when the fielders try to destroy the batsman's concentration by making pointed remarks, frequently personal and sometimes close to slander. When I was batting I loved it when the bowler or fielders would try to sledge me. I always ignored them and the more they got no reaction the more infuriated and frustrated they got. The bowlers nearly always bowled more wildly.

There was one particular game when a fast bowler said to me, 'The next ball will knock your head off.' One of the weapons of fast bowlers is that they can bowl at your head with the intention of intimidating you. This could affect your footwork and anticipation for the next ball. I looked blankly at him and he almost screamed, 'Did you hear what I said?' I gave him a wry smile. The next ball was indeed at my head.

There are two things you can do with a 'bouncer' – hook it or get out of the way. You can't think; it's instinctive. I was half expecting it and when it came I hooked it over a huge oak tree past the boundary and into the road. It was the best shot I have ever played in a 45-year cricket career. I still dream about that shot. I said nothing, but inside I was high fiving everybody and punching the air.

People are different on and off the field and after the game the fast bowler came up to me. 'Great shot,' he said. 'You are certainly the coolest customer I've ever played against.' I thanked him.

If you win, do so graciously. Watch the truly great sportspeople. They are nearly always self-deprecating and complimentary about their opponents. The same with good losers. They don't blame the referee or bad luck. They maintain their dignity. Respect your opponent, win or lose. As Grantland Rice said:

'For when the one great scorer comes to mark against your name he writes – not whether you won or lost – but how you played the game.'

Public Speaking

All my life I have been interested in public speaking. From my early teens, I read books on public speaking and went on courses. I relished any opportunity to speak in public. My one uncle was a Vaudeville artist. I think that I inherited the showbiz gene. I would make speeches at friends' birthday parties, weddings, barmitzvahs and in my work career.

One speech I made at a friend's wedding changed the rather serious mood to one of lightness and celebration. The bride's brother had been killed in a terrible accident nine months earlier. There was a sombre atmosphere permeating what should have been a joyful occasion. I didn't refer to the tragedy but focused solely on the couple and made a speech of humour and hope for the future. It included songs that blended into the speech and were sung by the pianist. The songs were 'Thank heaven for little girls,' 'The more we are together the happier we will be' and 'Will you still need me, will you still feed me, when I'm 64.' It was the year that man landed on the moon and the final part of the speech compared the wedding to the launching of a rocket ship to the moon. The last sentence was, 'May the final destination be The Sea of Tranquillity.' The whole audience laughed and started to relax, including the bride's parents. Until the moment of the speech they had been ambivalent, not knowing how to hide their still raw grief and yet wanting to celebrate their daughter's great day.

They weren't recording the proceedings at the wedding because they were concerned that the references to their son would be too painful. After the speech they asked me if I would go to the pianist's studio and record the speech. The atmosphere of the laughter and applause were missing, but they frequently used to listen to the speech. Something like Jonathan Sacks' 'Good News' file.

As the investment manager of L&G, I was required to give presentations to our clients on what I thought of the economy and the investment markets. This was the shop window of the company and the business depended almost entirely on the presentation (assuming of course that our investment returns were reasonable). I treated every presentation as a public speech and prepared thoroughly. After every presentation the company got new business.

I was invited to speak at the *Financial Mail* Investment Conference in 1980. Although L&G was a minnow in the fund management business in South Africa we had had the best returns for three years in a row. This wasn't well known, but with that record I had earned the right to be invited. The *Financial Mail* is the pre-eminent business weekly in South Africa.

There was standing room only for my speech, which was attended by more than 700 people. The conference took place over two days and, apart from the opening address by the Governor of the Reserve Bank, no other speaker drew more than 300 attendees. After that speech, the business of L&G trebled in the next three months and kept growing rapidly. The editor of the *Financial Mail* said that in 15 years of the conference he had never heard such a well-researched and well-delivered speech. It was written up in all the newspapers and publications and I became a household name. I was also invited to appear on television later on.

That conference was a pivotal moment in my career. From that one speech I went from obscurity to prominence.

I was suddenly known by every pension fund manager and director of every public company in South Africa. I was seen as an 'expert' and my credibility went sky high. There were a number of international guests there who also made contact with me and I became good friends with an American fund manager with whom I did business in later years. In addition I gained the respect of my competitors. When I started New Bernica I needed no introduction and most of the large institutions invested in my company.

Another example of one speech catapulting someone into the limelight was the poem read by Amanda Gorman at the inauguration of President Biden. She became a media sensation overnight and added one million followers to her social media account.

Public speaking is designed to influence people. In fact, most of what we say is intended to influence people, especially when it comes to seduction. I loved the speeches of great leaders – J.F. Kennedy, Winston Churchill, Martin Luther King Jr, among others. These speeches had the power to bring about huge changes in the world. Martin Luther King's powerful speech about 'I have a dream' still reverberates after 55 years. Unfortunately, powerful communication can also be destructive – Adolf Hitler and Josef Stalin harnessed their oratorical skills to whip up mass hysteria and hatred.

What distinguishes all outstanding leaders is the ability to communicate effectively. You can have the most brilliant speech, but if it is delivered in a monotone, it will have no impact. I believe that a major part of my success in life was due to my ability to speak well in public. I practised my speeches until I knew them almost by heart. I usually spoke without notes, which is very impressive, but not always necessary.

I would urge you to learn to speak in public, no matter how reticent you may feel about it. Steel yourself to do it. I can guarantee it will serve you in great stead. Even if you never have to make a major speech the training will give you confidence in your everyday interactions.

At the end of the book, you will find my 'Guidelines for Speakers' based on my experiences. I hope that it's helpful.

Racism, Sexism and Other Prejudices

I think I have been fortunate. Although, like everybody, I probably have inbuilt biases, from an early age I was aware of them and therefore was better able to control my feelings. The result was that I taught myself to respect everybody and treat all people as equally as possible.

At the height of Apartheid, in 1965, I was an audit clerk at a clothing company, in a suburb called Doornfontein. Close to the factory was a public park with a cricket net. One of the invoice clerks was a black man called Archie Hoko. Archie played cricket in Soweto and we used to talk about cricket. One day, I suggested that we go to Nugget Park at lunchtime and play in the net. I brought my kit and off we went.

Archie said he thought we were getting unwelcome stares from some people because the park was officially for whites only. I told him to ignore it and we continued to play at lunchtimes. To me he was just another fellow cricketer.

Our gardener, Elias Ngobeni, was once attacked outside our house. I could see that he was bleeding and I brought him in and cleaned him up before taking him to the hospital. My mother thought that it was a dangerous thing to do because his attackers may have still been in the garden. To me, he was just a person who needed treatment and I had to make sure that he was alright. He couldn't thank me enough.

I was very friendly with a Chinese boy at school. After school, we did accountancy together and he often came to my house. One day, in 1963, he invited me to his house for dinner. He lived in a very poor area in a place called Newclare, next to the black township, Soweto. My uncle took me. I thought nothing of it. At our 25th anniversary celebration in London he and his wife came from Toronto for the function. He told my sons that he was always sceptical of white people in Apartheid South Africa, but just the fact that I came to dinner convinced him of my sincerity. We've been the closest of friends for 61 years.

I have never, as far as I can recall, used any derogatory language about gender, race or religion either in public or private.

In 1976, I captained the Transvaal Junior Board cricket XI. In those days, the cricket leagues were 'mixed' and there were Indian teams and one from Soweto.

In my Board XI there were black and Indian players. I treated all the players fairly and respectfully. One of the Indian players commented on the way I handled the team. He said that he felt welcome, included and equal. This was fairly unusual for 1976 in South Africa.

I tell these stories to illustrate that I believe that every person should be treated on their merits. Instead of applying preconceived prejudices I always separate the person from their colour, religion, gender or sexual orientation. If I like or dislike someone it is based solely on whether we get on as people. I try to understand where they are coming from. I dislike aggressive people whatever their colour or orientation.

As a 76-year-old, white male, who lived during the unacceptable and unforgivable events that took place during the era that was Apartheid, I acknowledge the unfair treatment that all 'non-whites' were faced with. I recognise that I was given opportunities that other marginalised units of society and discriminated parties were not. South Africa is doing all that it can to repair the damage. It is our responsibility as a society, both in South Africa and the world at large, to teach all those around us to spread love, not hate. If we bear witness to such hate taking place, it is incumbent on us to take a stand and to fight for what is right. As Archbishop Desmond Tutu once said:

'If you are neutral in situations of injustice, you have chosen the side of the oppressor.'

Whatever applies to racism also applies to the LGBT community, women, black people, white men, old people, young people, foreigners, disabled, obese and mentally challenged people. Always be kind and understanding and never make fun of them in public or in private. Never generalise about any group, such as 'All men are misogynists'.

NEVER, EVER write a racial or sexist epithet on any social media platform. These words live forever. Whatever your feelings about these subjects, in 10 or 20 years' time, you can be pilloried. People have been forced to resign from jobs because of a casual remark years previously. An English footballer, who himself is black, made what he thought was an innocuous joke about the coronavirus that referenced a Chinese man. The English Football Association charged him with misconduct and bringing the game into disrepute.

One misguided or careless remark can be like Moses striking the rock. God told him to speak to the rock. He was excluded from entering the Promised Land. If you catch yourself about to make a racist or sexist joke, stop yourself, even if you think that it's funny. I would say that it is fine to say something like, 'I condemn all terrorist attacks.'

If you are the subject of a personal attack because of your race or gender, respond vigorously. However, try not to fall into the trap of lumping the perpetrator in a broad generalisation. It's usually better to attack the statement and only if necessary a particularly obnoxious individual. Remember that the person is really only talking about himself and is saying nothing about your race or gender.

Cults and Sects

At the time of my barmitzvah in 1957, our charismatic rabbi, Dr Abt, was accepting of his largely secular but traditional congregation. He did try to instil Jewishness into the youth. He started what he called a 'breakfast minyan' on a Sunday morning. It was for teenagers and consisted of morning prayers followed by a breakfast provided by the mothers. There would be a lesson and the whole service and breakfast lasted about 90 minutes.

I decided that I should become observant and so for three years I went to synagogue every morning and evening, kept Shabbat and kosher, and observed the Festivals. I wasn't fanatical, but quietly observant. Dr Abt was encouraging, but didn't try to control anyone. If any of his breakfast minyan attendees 'lapsed', he wasn't critical or scolding. I never felt part of a 'sect' where the only way was his way.

This phase ended when I went to university and I attended lectures on a Friday evening and on Saturday mornings. Clearly, I just wasn't that committed. I felt religion had no place for individual expression unless that expression complied with the laid-down laws. When I gave it up, I still identified with being Jewish, but felt released.

In my opinion, Haredi (ultra-Orthodox Jews) sects are potentially dangerous. It is extremely difficult to escape them. They seek to control your every movement and almost enslave the members of their communities. There are organisations in Israel and New York that specifically try to help people get away from them. The same applies to other sects such as the Moonies and many others.

It is fine to have heroes and people you look up to. By all means, follow them. But as soon as anybody says that if you stop following them, something bad will happen to you, get out. Run away as far as you can. A true leader will give you the choice whether to follow or not. There are many instances where cults have destroyed individuals and even whole families because the leader has a hold over the vulnerable members. One terrible instance was the Jonestown massacre in 1978 where the charismatic, self-styled 'Reverend' Jim Jones ordered 900 of his followers to commit suicide by cyanide poisoning, which they did. This number included 300 children.

Any sect or cult that uses mind-controlling techniques is to be avoided at all costs. More particularly if they ask you for money on an ongoing basis. If you wish, be part of a group of like-minded people. However, as soon as they try to obligate you to stay, leave immediately. I've got friends whose children joined sects and now refuse to see them. In fact, one friend's daughter took out a court injunction against her parents not to contact her or her children. True leaders, like Jiddu Krishnamurti, will always say:

'This is my way. If you like what you see, follow me. If you don't, you are free to move on.'

It's all about control. As with any personal relationship, you should be wary of people who want to control you. That doesn't mean to say that you shouldn't be totally loyal to a cause, but only if you do it of your own free will.

Don't be fooled by charismatic leaders – they have their own agendas. This applies to fanatical religious cults, be they Jewish, Muslim, Christian or otherwise. In my view a truly spiritual religious leader will be respectful of other religions.

Living a religious, orthodox life may be your choice, but don't try to force it on anyone else.

In the context of cults or sects I include fanatical or extreme quasi-political groups on the far right and far left – particularly if they threaten physical damage to property or violence. They may think that they have just causes, but in reality they have their own narrow and possibly pernicious agendas, which the vast majority don't adhere to. Any organisation that espouses violence is, by definition, a violent organisation. If they can be violent to any group they will have no hesitation in being violent to you if you cross them.

Coping with Illness

I have been in excellent health for most of my life, except for the thyroid and prostate cancers. I was fortunate that the thyroid cancer was largely dormant for six years from 2002 to 2008. After my thyroid operation in 2001, my vocal cord was paralysed and I could only speak in a high pitched whisper for three years. I had an operation to correct it. Unfortunately, the cancer came back aggressively and in 2009 I was put on a chemotherapy drug for 19 months. There were difficult side effects such as diarrhoea, high blood pressure, fatigue, pain in my feet and dyspepsia. At the same time, I was diagnosed with prostate cancer and was faced with difficult new side effects.

Everyone and every circumstance is different. This is what worked for me. When I had my prostate cancer operation in 2009, I was in a huge amount of pain and discomfort, attached to a catheter for two weeks. I was feeling terrible and decided that I had to articulate a 'strategy for coping' – a plan.

My attitude made it much easier for me to adapt to the potentially harsh reality and Roni and my family weren't stressed more than would be expected in the circumstances.

My friend, Terry Cooper, also gave me the following mantra.

Look in the mirror and say aloud:

- ➢ I love you exactly as you are
- ➢ I care for you in this difficult time
- ➢ I am strong
- ➢ I will get through this.

It is difficult enough to love oneself 'exactly as you are' and it's even more difficult when you are feeling and looking under the weather. Saying the mantra was like giving a nurturing hug to a wounded child. The child in me felt understood and protected. I felt compassionate towards myself. I would do it four or five times a day, sometimes with tears in my eyes. It always made me feel better for the moment.

'This difficult time' also acknowledges that it is, indeed, a difficult time. No point in glossing this over with a bland 'everything will be okay.' It is reality.

When I said 'I'm strong' and 'I will get through this' I gritted my teeth. My determination was accessing my deepest inner strength. Like being on the last leg of climbing Mount Everest. Whatever the pain, you have to get to the top.

I give you my strategy for coping with my cancer and other major setbacks, not necessarily medical.

Count your blessings

When I was going through the agony of radiotherapy on my throat I found it very difficult to swallow. I used to wake up in the morning and think to myself, 'When should I have my first swallow?' It was usually in my shower. I found it extremely difficult to eat and had to have soft foods and clear soup. I started counting my blessings – family, friends, work, home, financial security, the fact that I was healthy in other respects and many other blessings – and that made me feel better. You can keep a 'gratitude diary' and write down three things that you are grateful for, on a daily basis. I focussed on what I have got, rather than what I didn't have. When I was thinking of all the good things in my life, it took my mind off my pain.

Never complain or wallow in self-pity

Complaining just makes the person you are complaining to feel helpless. Indulging in self-pity just makes *you* feel helpless. This is different from an honest statement of fact that you don't feel so good. I tried never to complain, but sometimes the pain was so great that I just burst into tears.

Accept the situation

If you really can't change it, accept it. Acceptance eases your pain and brings your body and mind to the same place. Sometimes it is very difficult to accept a situation and then all you can do is experience the pain and wait for it to pass. Recognise that you can't shoulder charge the Great Wall of China.

Remember the power of a sense of humour

When I couldn't swallow, sometimes I would start crying. I got over it by saying that if I couldn't get moisture in my mouth, at least I could get it in my eyes. When I could hardly speak, I used to say, 'Don't let the softness of my voice detract from the seriousness of my purpose.' I would wear very brightly coloured shirts and say, 'The loudness of my shirt makes up for the softness of my voice.'

Even at the height of my pain and discomfort I used to listen to recordings of a BBC program called *I'm Sorry I Haven't A Clue*. It is a humorous panel game on BBC 4. A friend sent me a box set. I laughed so much that I forgot the pain.

Take responsibility

I took responsibility for what I was going through. I avoided saying things like, 'Why me?' I had to get on with trying to heal myself

Listening to music

Music is important in my life. When I sit at my computer I have music playing softly in the background. Either BBC Radio 2 or I listen to songs of the thirties, forties, fifties and sixties on YouTube. My grandchildren call it 'Grandpa's music' as they chuckle when I put it on. I'm quite sure that most of my readers will never have heard of Benny Goodman, The Dorsey Brothers, Glenn Miller, The Platters, The Ink Spots or Artie Shaw. My absolute favourite vocalists are Ella Fitzgerald and Matt Monroe.

Although not a strategy in itself, I was extremely fortunate to have the untiring support of Roni and my family and friends. Cancer is a disease that affects the whole family and when I was feeling vulnerable and weak I was grateful that Roni was a rock. Her strength was a spur for me to maintain as cheerful a disposition as possible. One of us had to be really strong when I was so vulnerable. No point in her also collapsing.

After an Operation

I have had five major operations in the past 18 years to deal with thyroid cancer and prostate cancer. I developed a strategy to overcome the fear and pain. I now tell this to everybody I know who is going in for an operation.

Before my thyroid cancer operation in 2001, the anaesthetist took me to the Intensive Care Unit and explained to me what would happen when I came round. I would be attached to a number of tubes and drains and my blood pressure would be taken every couple of minutes. I was terrified that I would feel claustrophobic and so I formulated the following mantra, which I practised to myself for an hour before the operation. I determined to repeat it as soon as I came round.

- ➤ Stay calm
- ➤ I'm safe
- ➤ I'm in good hands
- ➤ Surrender to the process (let go)
- ➤ I'm strong
- ➤ I will get through this.

When I came round there was an oxygen mask on my face and I had no voice at all because the operation had paralysed my one vocal cord. I mentally repeated the mantra at regular intervals, and I didn't feel claustrophobic or fearful. There is something comforting about feeling safe and in good hands.

The operation was supposed to have taken two hours. However, the tumour had spread and the surgeon spent an extra two hours trying to save the vocal chord, which he was unable to do. Roni and David came to see me. They were quite frantic when the operation went on for so long. David was in a terrible state to see me in my terrible state.

The next morning, he visited me before work. I decided that no matter how bad I was feeling, I wouldn't add to his fear. He came into the ICU and gingerly asked how I was. 'Tickety boo, Davey. I had a good night and I'm not in too much pain.' His face lit up with huge relief.

I gave this mantra to two friends of mine, one of whom had a heart-valve replacement. When he came round from the operation, the machine was breathing for him. He started to panic. He then remembered the mantra; the most important thing for him was to surrender to the process. He said that he let go, which stopped his panic. He reckoned that it saved his life. He gives the mantra to every person who is having an operation.

My other friend had a serious back operation and also started to panic until he remembered the mantra. The most important things to him were, 'I'm safe' and 'I'm in good hands'. He too believed that the mantra saved him significant psychological damage.

Bereavement

In 1970, I was away in London when the father of a good friend died. When I got back to Johannesburg, I heard the news. I didn't know what to say to my friend and avoided calling him. After a week or so I called him. He asked if I knew that his father had died and I lied that I hadn't. I felt quite ashamed.

There will be times when your friends suffer bereavement in their family. Usually it's of an ageing parent, but not always. This is a very difficult time for them and it's often hard to know what to say or do. It might be tough for you to face them, but the worst thing to do is to stay away, as I did.

As mentioned earlier, we had friends who lost a seven-year-old son in a car accident. The husband was injured and spent six weeks in a hospital in Bloemfontein. We lived in Johannesburg, but Roni and I spent almost all six weeks at a hotel close to the hospital.

In times of bereavement friends and family need the most support that you can give.

> At these very difficult times, always be available to do whatever your friend or family may need.
> Where possible attend the funeral. People will deeply appreciate your being there.

Chapter 5

Money

Money was, and is, very important to me (and to everyone). Oscar Wilde said,

> **'When I was young I thought that money was the most important thing in life. Now that I'm old I know that it is.'**

On many occasions in my life I felt that I didn't have enough money to buy the things I wanted. 'Enough' is whatever you think is enough for you. My father went through numerous iterations of having money and losing nearly all his money. We moved from a small house in a solidly middle-class suburb (Parkwood) to a large double-storey house with a tennis court and garden in a smarter suburb (Saxonwold). When I was 12 my father then lost most of his money and we moved to a small residential hotel in a densely populated area (Berea) for a while.

This was followed by a smallish apartment in Killarney and after a few years, my father made some money and when I was 15, we moved to a beautiful house in upmarket Riviera. We stayed there for a number of years and then my father lost money again, sold the house and moved back to an apartment in Killarney. He then made money and moved back to an apartment in Riviera. In 1973, due to a swindle, my father went bankrupt and lost everything. He spent the last years of his life in a small apartment in a poor neighbourhood

I have been through many financial ups and downs. Until 1987, I barely had any savings but had a good job. In 1985, funds were really short and we cancelled a holiday because we simply could not afford it. In 1989, we sold our company and for the first time in my life I had some savings. We moved from Johannesburg to London, but for four years I couldn't get a job and we lived off our savings.

In 1994, I started a new company in South Africa and in the next 10 years, I managed to make enough money to retire. It wasn't a huge sum and I am by no means mega wealthy, but fortunately I know what it is to be comfortable.

If you are lucky enough to be rich, there will be many people who will be envious and will try to disparage you. This envy has nothing to do with you; it is a reflection of the envious person. 'Beware the cripple ...'

Also, don't be ashamed of spending some of your money thinking that it will make you envied. 'Never limp in front of a cripple ...' Huge conspicuous consumption may be inappropriate in certain circumstances. I have friends with flamboyant personalities who like to spend extravagantly and have lavish parties. They are just being themselves.

Without sufficient money there is misery and deprivation. Having no money is one of the most debilitating experiences that one can have. It can negatively impact a romantic relationship too. I think the saying rings true:

'When poverty creeps under the door, love flies out of the window.'

In today's world, it may be hip to be left-leaning and many university students and young people lean that way. They will talk about social equality and level playing fields which all sound enticing and make them feel good. I have always been in the political centre, but even as a teenager I knew how my father struggled with money on various occasions. I determined from a young age that I needed to make money. I strongly believe in free enterprise where it's fine to be rich. At the same time it is incumbent on the government to protect the most vulnerable in society and create equal opportunities wherever possible.

There is no fairness in life. Is it 'fair' that one person has a better voice than most others? Is it fair that one person can run faster than everyone else? Should we handicap the fastest runners by making them run with weights? I try to celebrate people's success and strive for my own. I tend to ignore people who cavil over 'privilege' or somebody's 'unfair' start in life. I don't apologise for who I am or where I come from. I just want to be the very best I can be. That applies to making as much money as I can, in an honest endeavour. I don't feel guilty about living in a nice house or driving a good car. Actually, I drive a Honda – I've never been a car person. My view is that the 'sin' is to envy these things.

The journeyman who lives in a modest suburb, has a loving family and is in good health is far better off than the multi-millionaire whose children shun him.

Wealth carries great influence. Doors open to the wealthy, because most people respect money. As the character Tevye says in the *Fiddler on the Roof* song 'If I Were a Rich Man', 'When you're rich they think you really know'. It is far easier to arrange service providers and get things done when you have money. If there is a medical crisis, money can get help quickly. My first cancer medication was not available on the National Health Service. It is expensive and wasn't covered by private insurance at the time. Had I not had the money, I possibly wouldn't be alive today.

Money can do an enormous amount of good. Think of great philanthropists like Bill Gates and Warren Buffett, who give billions to fighting disease, poverty and the lack of education. One of my regrets in life is that I wasn't super-rich, because then I could have given most of the money away. Generosity is a most appealing characteristic. Meanness is ugly.

Having money carries responsibility. It is equally important that one retains the values of integrity, respect and humility. Just because you have money does not automatically mean that you should be shown respect or deference. You have to earn it by treating everyone with respect and making sure that they retain their dignity. For men, money does not entitle you to grope women or expect them to do sexual favours. That's just boorish behaviour and deserves contempt.

When you're 'young' money is really for spending. As a bachelor, whatever money I earned, I spent. There wasn't much left over for savings. When I earned a bit more than I needed for monthly expenses, I invested the difference in shares. I was fortunate because I worked as a stockbroker, so investments came naturally to me.

My strong suggestion to you is that whenever you have excess cash, invest in equities. If you are able to analyse individual stocks and have a penchant for investing then clearly you can pick your own stocks. The stock market fluctuates, sometimes wildly. But in the long term, returns are far better than those obtainable on fixed interest securities. Cash should only be a short-term investment. It is only valuable if asset prices are falling. A long-term holding of cash will be highly detrimental because inflation will erode its value. Furthermore, there will be the lost opportunity cost of being invested in equities.

If you don't have a particular interest in stock picking or analysis, there are two things you can do. You can find a good fund manager who takes money on a monthly basis or you can invest in index tracking funds. The argument against index tracking funds is that you are buying 'bad' stocks in the index as well as good ones. Some fund managers are able to do better than the indices on a fairly regular basis. If you can find such managers, by all means invest with them. By definition, the index will be the average of all returns. I have found that I am satisfied with doing as well as the index.

I cannot overstate the importance of making sound investments over the course of your life. It enabled me to spend my retirement years, when I was unable to work, in relative comfort. Whilst I said that I didn't want to be prescriptive there is one piece of advice that I'd like to give you that is *essential*. Whenever you buy or sell shares always do so 'at best.' Never give a limit. When I was inexperienced, I once gave an order to buy a stock at 120. The price quoted was 119.50 to 120.50. The next sale was 120.50 and then 125. Now I was upset. I upped the limit to 125, but the price moved again. I ended up paying 140 two days later. It's the same on the way down. If a share is worth 120, it's worth 122 and vice versa.

My yoga teacher, Mani Finger, once said to me that kicking the 'football of life' on the stock exchange is actually no different to meditating in the mountains of India. Everything depends on your inner feelings. If you meditate in the mountains of India but wish that you were making money on the stock exchange, it would be waste of time. At the same time, you can be very rich and live a sincere, mindful and honest life. As an illustration he told me this story:

'A man went looking for the most respected swami in India. He wanted to sit at his feet and learn. He walked half the length of the country and arrived at the swami's house. He was shocked at what he found. The swami lived in a large beautiful house with rolling lawns and lavish furnishings. He believed that the swami, who, as spiritual leader to his people should be setting an example, was living in the lap of luxury. He angrily said to the swami, "How can you live with so much materialism. You're nothing but a fraud," and he left.

'Fortunately, he knew that the second most famous swami lived nearby and he found his way to his home. It was modest house and the swami lived in the simplest of surroundings. There was practically no furniture and the swami sat crossed legged on the floor. The man said, "I walked halfway across India to find the greatest teacher and I landed up at the rich swami's residence. I realised what a fraud he

155

was and I came here. I can see that you are a man of deep spirituality living this ascetic life. I want to follow you."

'The swami thought for a moment and said, "That other swami is one of the greatest sages in the world. He lives like he does because he's impervious to it. I live like this because I'm impervious to it."'

Chapter 6

The World of Work

A job is one of the most precious things in the world. Without work, your life is likely to be empty. Unemployment is the scourge that destroys families and causes great hardship. Having no job is a big thing in life.

People often complain about their work, but I recommend that you always take your job seriously and strive to do your best at all times. When you don't feel like getting up in the morning try 'Oh boy, work.' 'Oh boy, contributing.' 'Oh boy, earning my keep.' Every job is important. There is a song from the Second World War, 'The Thingummy Bob', by Gordon Thompson and David Heneker, about a woman who works in a factory in a rote job. It goes:

'I can't pretend to be
A great celebrity
But still I'm quite important in my way
The job I have to do may not sound much to you
But all the same, I'm very proud to say

I'm the girl that makes the thing
that drills the hole that holds the ring
that drives the rod that turns the knob
that works the thingummy bob'

Even if you take a vac job as a waiter or barman, put your heart and soul into it. The people you work with will notice everything you do. From an early age, your attitude to work will be a precursor to whether you will succeed or not in later life.

When I was 16, I helped out a friend's father at a trade show. He sold soft toys, such as teddy bears. One particular client had asked for a toy that wasn't easily accessible. I rummaged through the stock at the back of the stall and eventually found it. The customer was happy and commented to my friend's father on my willingness to 'go the extra mile'. I got an additional 10 shillings, which in 1960 was a lot of money! In today's money it would be worth around £40 (R800, $52). It may have been a simple job, but I gave it focus and I always remembered the reward for hard work

One of the biggest problems facing young people leaving school is what to do with their lives. If you are lucky, you will know that you want to be an IT specialist, lawyer, beautician, doctor, nurse, teacher, social worker or artist, etc. and you can study accordingly. Or you may want to go straight into the world of work.

I was particularly good with numbers and so it was natural for me to study accountancy. After I qualified, I knew that I didn't want to be an auditor, but my degree enabled me to find jobs as an accountant in business. My father was a stockbroker and when I was 24, he asked me to join him. That set me on the path of being an investor and I was fortunate enough to find my niche.

I left stockbroking after seven years and became an investment manager for L&G. From there I started formalised private equity in South Africa.

Throughout my career, I tried to stay passionate about the business. There were tricky situations and major setbacks, such as deals going sour, differences with our partners, the threat of litigation, stock market crashes and poor trading conditions. There were occasions, like the crash of 1987, when I thought of giving it all up, but I persevered and kept the end goal in sight – like marathon runners who force themselves through the pain barrier.

Your work defines you to a large extent. The London chapter of an international business networking group, Young Presidents' Organisation (YPO), of which I am a member, did some charitable work for the Save the Children Fund. The patron was Princess Anne. The chapter was invited for drinks and snacks at Buckingham Palace. Princess Anne made a point of meeting every member. The first questions she asked were, 'Where are you from and what do you do?'

Consider the people you know. You will immediately associate them with their work, if they have started work. Ken is a mechanic, Sheila is an accountant, Timothy works at the sweet factory, Jeremy is a footballer, etc. If you are unsure about what you want to do, consult a career-guidance specialist. There are so many options today – vocations and careers that were never imagined even five years ago. Explore all the alternatives that might appeal to you and take the utmost care to find what you think will be the best path for you. Unless you are very lucky, through inheritance or winning the lottery, you have to make money to survive.

Present yourself in the best possible light, but never lie on your CV. If it is discovered, your reputation will be ruined. Even if you've been in a job for a considerable time, if the lie surfaces you are likely to be fired. A good friend stated on his CV that he took a commerce degree, but in fact he only finished three years of the four-year course. He became the chief executive of a large subsidiary of the company. A few years later it was discovered that he hadn't completed the degree. He was summarily dismissed.

If you are in a job it is usually best to stay in the job before taking on another job. You may be unhappy or want a greater challenge, which happens all the time. Being out of a job can put you under pressure and could affect how you approach new potential employers.

One of my mentees was a young woman of around 28. She was doing well in her job, but wanted a greater challenge. She submitted her CV to an agency. In the meantime I advised her that she should keep up her high standards. The company was still paying her and she had a duty to do the best that she could. Not doing so was tantamount to stealing. The result was that she did so well that before she found something new she was promoted. She still wanted to move, but the promotion made her job prospects even better. She was very ambitious and eventually started her own business.

When you go for a job interview, prepare extremely well. There is nearly all you need to know about even the smallest businesses through the internet and social media. The interviewer will be impressed by your diligence and knowledge.

Be enthusiastic. If you need to submit something in writing beforehand make the tone upbeat. Show that you are excited about getting the job and how you think you may go about it. Some people don't want to sound desperate and that's good. I hired a number of people in my life. I never gave a second interview to anyone who didn't give the impression that it was really important to them.

Roni and I needed a personal assistant and housekeeper. We interviewed four people. One was from the Philippines. She was bubbly and said that she was confident that she could do the job well. She also said that she was willing to learn the intricacies. She had a cheerful disposition, without being over the top. We hired her.

She was quite inexperienced and Roni trained her with kindness, but firmness. In the 15 years that she was with us she became world class. She used to do the shopping. We never told her what to buy. If she saw an empty toothpaste tube in the trash she bought toothpaste. She had my credit card. I never checked the statement.

When we left the country I wrote her a reference that she framed. She had a number of job offers and was able to choose the best one.

If you can't get work that you think you may love, love the work you get. Keep trying to improve. The greater the mastery, the greater the pleasure. This applies in all walks of life.

I found that maximum efficiency was achieved when I planned my next day the night before. My desk was always neat with ongoing papers laid out neatly on the right-hand side of the desk. Later in life, I made sure that my inbox had no more than 10 emails.

I was never afraid to consult others either in-house or externally. I was happy to collaborate or ask for assistance when I needed it.

However, when I was expected to know something, I always tried to work it out before seeking advice. Usually I had the answers, but sometimes not. I didn't feel that I lost face by approaching colleagues. External advisers were always pleased to earn the fees.

In 1979, Bjorn Borg won his fourth Wimbledon title. I was at a restaurant and he walked in with his entourage, including his coach. Another epiphany. It struck me that if the best in the world needed a coach, what about us simple mortals? I changed my entire management style to be more of a coach and mentor. Instead of giving orders I asked questions so that my people would explore more and find the answers. They all flourished and I was well liked and respected.

I was particularly lucky with my 'unofficial' mentors. One was Ken Whyte, the chairman of New Bernica who was also one of the senior partners at Coopers and Lybrand (now PricewaterhouseCoopers). He was one of the founders of Impala Platinum and so was highly successful. The 'mentorship' was never defined as such. I just used to metaphorically sit at his feet and learn. My other mentor was Derek Keys, who was the executive chairman of General Mining (Gencor), one of the largest mining houses in South Africa. He later became the Minister of Finance. We would arrange to walk around the lake at one of Johannesburg's large parks. Mainly he spoke and I soaked up everything he said like a sponge.

There are many organisations that provide mentorship. You could benefit greatly from having a mentor. The chief executive of L&G was very forward looking. His style was to say that everyone needed to question anything that they wanted to. His focus was on people innovating and coming up with original thoughts. He used to say that it's fine if you failed. In 1976 it was *avant garde*. The result was a lively debate at the highest level of management with everyone speaking their minds. It led to a golden period for the company.

I never took anything personally when it came to 'negative' feedback. I separated the feedback from the person and looked at it dispassionately. If it was justified, I changed whatever I had to. If not, I argued my case calmly and without acrimony. The way to collaborate is to focus entirely on the problem and not on the person. You need to lose your ego in looking for the best solution to the problem at hand. American President Harry S. Truman said:

> *'It's amazing what you can accomplish if you don't care who gets the credit.'*

I always tried to be cooperative, where possible, at work, because we were a team and were all working towards the same goal. However, I wouldn't be pushed around if asked to do something outside my normal activities, such as filling in for a colleague when I knew that he was too lazy to do the task. I wasn't defensive but stood firm and stated my case calmly with a measured tone of voice and I very seldom got angry (although anger is sometimes appropriate – see 'Anger').

A common phenomenon experienced in the workplace is known as the 'imposter syndrome'. You feel that you're not good enough for the job and you're just waiting to be found out. I had this most of my working life and sometimes still do today! I tried to overcome it by telling myself that

162

I was selected because I must have had some competency. The people who selected me believed in me. I told myself that I was as entitled as anyone else to be there. I could never fully get rid of the syndrome, so I just got on with the job to the best of my ability. I took pride in my small everyday successes and made plans to overcome the setbacks.

It is estimated that 70% of people suffer from the syndrome at some point in their careers. Great stars like Meryl Streep and Tom Hanks have spoken about it. If it happens that you get this feeling, remember that you are not alone. I'm not suggesting that you should just 'get over it'. Just 'get on' with it (life and your job).

It is important to be reliable. If you say you'll do something, do it properly and on time. I have always been that way, although I occasionally do something unexpected or supposedly 'out of character' – as long as it's not dishonest or damaging to others. You should always be reliable, but not one-dimensional or predictable. It adds a little mystery and makes you interesting.

The workplace is a world of complex relationships. People's work is their livelihood and they will be very protective of their jobs and position. You could be seen as a threat or an ally, but either way you need to get on well with your colleagues and employers as far as possible. All the general principles of relationships (see Chapter 2) apply in the workplace too.

When I was the investment manager of L&G, the British managing director was due to go back to the UK, to be replaced by a South African. There were four managers at my level who were in line for the job. Investments had done particularly well (we were the top-performing institution five years in a row). All our insurance products were sold on the back of the investment performance. I was close to the managing director and had an excellent relationship with the chief executive and the chairman of the UK parent company. It was clear that I was the front runner for the appointment.

The marketing manager was also a strong contender. The company was doing particularly well and the business had more than quintupled in the six years that I was there. Naturally the marketing manager was taking the credit, even though the marketing was all based on the excellent investment performance. Foolishly, instead of embracing me as a colleague who was doing very well for the team, he tried to undermine me in order to get the top job. It's like a member of the English football team trying to undermine the captain, Harry Kane.

Every year there was a sales conference for all the salespeople and top management. It normally happened at a smart resort and it was meant to introduce new products and to reward the top salespeople. I was always one of the main speakers, not because I could advise the agents, but so that I could keep them informed about the investments and how I saw the economy and the markets.

In 1980, the conference was due to be held at the Swazi Spa, a resort in Swaziland. The conferences normally took place over four days. Being a keynote speaker, I had always spoken on the first day of the conference. The marketing manager was responsible for the venue and for organising all aspects of the conference.

I received notification that the dates were 10-13 October. I noticed that 11 October was Yom Kippur – one of the holiest days in the Jewish calendar – and so, because of my affiliation, I could only join the conference on 12 October. I informed the marketing department that I could only make it on that date. Two members of the department were shocked. I was close to them and they knew that the salespeople liked me very much. They asked the marketing manager to change the date. He replied that there were only two Jewish people who would attend, so it shouldn't be a problem. He also said that the deposit had been paid and that it was too late to change the date.

I didn't take it personally and thought it was just an oversight on the part of the marketing manager. I was happy to come on the third day, but the two guys in the marketing department were adamant. They went to the managing director, who called in the marketing manager. He stood his ground. But the two said that if the dates weren't changed, they would resign. The managing director ordered that the dates be changed.

My strategy was to remain calm and almost detached. I didn't take umbrage or get angry. In my view, that could only have caused open animosity and that could have been damaging to the company. My record spoke for itself. The marketing manager had nothing to attack. It was like him boxing in cotton wool. That doesn't mean to say that my reaction was the only correct one, but it worked for me. As it is, I don't like direct confrontation, unless it is absolutely necessary.

The marketing guys told me a few months later, that, in an unguarded moment, after a few drinks, the marketing manager admitted that he knew it was Yom Kippur. He also said that he thought he should get the top job.

The company was then taken over by a South African group and I left to start New Bernica. Needless to say, the marketing director did not become the managing director and shortly after the takeover, he left the company.

There are always tensions and differences in the workplace as well as strong loyalties and camaraderie. Even the top successful sports teams have complex differences in the dressing room. These have to be dealt with to work as a team and achieve success.

When the admin manager of L&G retired, I had to make a speech at his farewell. I said that every person should figuratively frame their day's work, hang it on the wall and sign it, like an artist. Sometimes you will feel proud of the work and sometimes not. I said that the admin manager's work would deserve a place in an art gallery. He was the Thomas Gainsborough of admin managers. He was so efficient that he could be proud of his contribution. He was a dour man, but after the speech he smiled broadly and became more effusive than I had ever seen him.

Every person is doing a job that is essential to the organisation and it should be acknowledged. Everybody wants to feel affirmed. An illustration from my own experience: I went to a laboratory to have bloods taken. The blood-taker was a very unprepossessing lady who was quite surly. When she inserted the needle she said, 'This may hurt a bit.' After she took the blood I smiled and said, 'Painless, absolutely painless.' A broad grin spread across her face. 'You've made my day,' she beamed. As they say in the song, 'Little things mean a lot.'

Negotiations

Negotiation is the fuel on which all commercial activity is driven. Not only in business, but in everyday life we want something from another person. Children negotiate almost exclusively at a jarring emotional level with their parents. 'Mommy, please can I have an ice cream?' 'Not before dinner.' 'But you gave Robert one yesterday at four o'clock. It's not fair.' None of this is said in a whisper.

In business, negotiations are usually conducted using reason and persuasive argument. 'The rent is too high. In the three previous deals done in the region the rents have gone down.' 'Those deals fail to take into account that our property has better infrastructure than the others.' Occasionally there is a brutal attack on the opposition, but that will most likely increase the conflict.

At a social level there are also negotiations. 'I'd like to go to see the latest Benedict Cumberbatch movie tonight. It got five stars and you know that he's my favourite actor.' 'Wouldn't you prefer to go to the swish new bistro? They have amazing lobster bisque. I really love it and there are few places you can get it.'

Whatever your vocation, it is essential that you learn to negotiate. Read books or take a course. You wouldn't drive a car before taking lessons. Before using a new cellphone you read the instructions. A wonderful movie on negotiation is *Draft Day* (2014, dir. Ivan Reitman) starring Kevin Costner.

In all negotiations it is imperative to prepare extensively. Know your facts and know your limits. Believe in yourself and trust your inner voice. I also used visualisations, similar to those used by athletes before a race.

In the most important business deal of my life the negotiation had reached a stalemate with each of us refusing to budge. I had read *Getting to Yes* (revised edition 2011, Baker and Taylor) by Roger Fisher and William Ury. I opened it randomly and landed on the page where Anwar Sadat, the iconic Egyptian leader, wanted to make peace with Israel. He called Menachem Begin, the Prime Minister of Israel, and arranged to address the Knesset (Israeli parliament).

I picked up the phone and said to the other party that we had to meet. I offered a concession that was important to him but was more cosmetic on our side. The deal was consummated and it was the making of my company. We never had a difference again.

John F. Kennedy said,

'We will never negotiate out of fear and we will never fear to negotiate.'

It has the same impact and validity 60 years later.

If you have the potential to reach a managerial position you need to be a good negotiator and a good leader, at whatever level you achieve. Read books and/or take courses on negotiation and on leadership.

Office Romances

> One in five people meets their life partner at work. This makes a lot of sense because of the intimate nature of one's job and the time spent at work. It is fine to date someone in your office, provided you comply with the rules of the firm and there is no conflict of interest. Usually, you should not date someone who works for you and who you may favour. Depending on the size of the company one of you should move to another department if possible.

> In today's world, where political correctness and allegations of sexual harassment can result in people losing their jobs (often unfairly), you need to know how to handle an office romance. Distinguish between flirtation and harassment. The natural inclination of people is a desire to connect with each other. Flirtation is where there is an obvious attraction between people and they both know it. Harassment, however, is when someone in a position of power makes advances or uses inappropriate language to a subordinate. Steve Easterbrook, the boss of burger giant McDonald's, had to resign in 2019 because he was having a relationship with a junior colleague, even though it was consensual and both were adults. At the time of writing, McDonald's is suing

for return of his severance payment. Most times it's men who harass women, but it's not always that way round.

- ➢ Harassment is also when a fellow employee, not necessarily a superior, makes advances or uses suggestive language or behaviour when there is no attraction between the parties.
- ➢ If you are the subject of harassment you should be firm, but, initially, not angry if you can avoid it.
- ➢ You should say that you are not happy with the unwanted attention and ask the person to desist.
- ➢ If he/she does persist, anger might be appropriate.
- ➢ If it still continues, it may be necessary to report the person, but that should be a last resort.
- ➢ If your boss asks you to sleep with him or her and promises you will get promoted, you should very firmly decline and tell him/her that if it happens again you will report it.
- ➢ If anyone touches you inappropriately, you should react angrily.
- ➢ You should never sexually harass anybody or take advantage of your position to get sexual favours.

Conclusion

I hope this book has provided some useful pointers of how you see and handle the big and less big things in life. I hope it has served as a catalyst for self-reflection and movement where you desire movement. Perhaps it has ignited a thirst to continue working on yourself and your awareness of others. Life is like a labyrinth. You never know where it is going to take you, but you do know that there is always a way through it. There is an enormous amount of literature on all of the subjects which I have touched upon briefly. Avail yourself of it.

I like Holocaust survivor and author Viktor Frankl's words about living in the moment:

> *'For the meaning of life differs from person to person, from day to day and from hour to hour. What matters, therefore, is not the meaning of life in general but rather the specific meaning of a person's life at a given moment.'*

I don't know the meaning of life; all I know is that at this moment, the big things in my life are my family, my health and that of my family, my friends and having enough money to last me and Roni for the remainder of our lives. I'm going to do my utmost to make the most of it – now.

American physician Oliver Wendell Holmes said:

'Most of us go to our graves with our music still inside us, unplayed.'

It's up to you, and you alone, to create your own symphonies. The question is:

What are you going to do differently tomorrow?

Good luck!

Guidelines for Speakers

Speak Brilliantly with Confidence and Authority

'In matters of great unimportance, it's style not sincerity that counts. In matters of great importance, it's style not sincerity that counts.'

Oscar Wilde

You are invited to make a speech. How should you go about it?

➢ Know and understand the **purpose** of the speech
➢ Think about and decide what you want to **achieve** with the speech
➢ Analyse the nature of the **audience/s** (there can be more than one 'audience' at any occasion, each with its own characteristics, and which may require different treatment)
➢ Think about and decide what you would like the audience to **think** and **feel**
➢ Think about and decide what you would like the audience to **do** after the speech (a great many speeches (and everyday conversations) are about how you can **persuade** people and **influence their behaviour**)
➢ Write down the **most important message** you want your audience to take away
➢ Write down the **key points** that you want to make

- ➤ **Plan** the speech with an outline of the beginning, middle and end and where the key points will fit in
- ➤ **Write** the speech, **refine** the speech, **practice** the speech, **deliver** the speech
- ➤ Speeches are there to:
  - Inform
  - Appeal for action - **persuade, influence behaviour**
  - Pay homage or respect
  - Introduce someone
  - Thank someone
  - **Entertain** (all speeches must entertain, whatever the purpose)

Audience

There can be many different audiences in the same room when you make a speech. Who is/are your various audience/s?

- ➤ Customers
- ➤ Suppliers
- ➤ Providers of finance
- ➤ Shareholders
- ➤ Family
- ➤ Spouse
- ➤ Parents
- ➤ Children
- ➤ Friends
- ➤ Guests at an important function
- ➤ The media
- ➤ Work colleagues
- ➤ Voters
- ➤ Ministers of religion
- ➤ Others

Is the speech directed to the audience/s you want to reach? Some aspects of the speech may appeal to one section of the audience, some parts to another.

Two elements of the speech:

- ➢ **Content**
  - Purpose
  - Mood
  - Structure
  - Feelings
  - Actions
  - Flow
  - Words
  - Time frame – all speeches have a finite time. Ensure you know how long you should be speaking for and keep to that time. Rough guide – 100/120 words a minute

- ➢ **Delivery**
  - Voice projection
  - Posture
  - Gestures
  - Props
  - Pace and rhythm
  - Appearance
  - Confidence

Content

'Life and death are on the tip of the tongue.'

- ➢ The content (every word, every gesture, every pause) of the speech must be totally directed towards fulfilling the objective and purpose of the speech

➢ Every speech must be carefully crafted and have a planned beginning, middle and end
➢ When writing the speech, whenever you think of something that you could include in the speech, write it down immediately (for instance in your shower you think of something clever or funny, as soon as you get out, write it down)
➢ Feel passionate and enthusiastic about the subject
➢ Understand why the audience should care about what you are saying – how does it affect them?
➢ Think about and decide what mood you want to create and write accordingly
  • Light
  • Frivolous
  • Romantic
  • Touchy/feely
  • Intellectual
  • Urgent
  • Serious
  • Sombre
➢ Start with an **attention-grabbing** sentence
  • The very first thing you say and how you say it is vital
  • You have 15 seconds to capture the audience
  • First sentence can be humorous or powerful or both
  • Very early on start with the purpose of the speech
  • Avoid:
    ○ Apologies
    ○ Explanations
    ○ Talking about yourself
    ○ Padding (if you have five minutes and use 50 unnecessary words you've lost 10% of your speech as well as losing your audience)
➢ You must have sincerity and, where appropriate, passion
➢ Speak from the heart
➢ Speak from your experience and talk about what you know about

(in researching some speeches you may need 10, 20, 50 or even 100 times or more knowledge as is actually contained in the content of the speech)

➤ Draw on all the resources you can – your own experiences and observations, experiences of others, news items – current or old, history, Shakespeare or other authors, the bible, television shows, movies, mythology, folk stories, nursery rhymes, quotation books, etc.

➤ Be yourself

➤ Use your imagination

➤ Experiment with different structures or words

➤ Use poetic licence (but never try to deceive people by using blatantly false information)

➤ Content should include some or most of the following, depending on the speech:

- Originality (can be what you say as well as the way you say something)
- Say things differently (e.g. instead of saying 'She is an extremely knowledgeable person', you could say, 'If you want information, ask Sheila, the human Google')
- Humour
  - Timing
  - The unexpected
  - Juxtaposition of the unexpected or unusual
  - Never humiliate anyone, but a funny story where someone can laugh at themselves can be effective – so long as it is not insulting
  - Humour (or satire) will be remembered longer and will bring home the message more than just words (like this sentence)
  - Puns – Sign outside a nudist colony 'Come in, we are never clothed'
  - Chiastic quotations – 'It's not the men in my life, it's the life in my men' Mae West. 'Never let a fool kiss you or a kiss fool you.'

- Alliteration – many words beginning with the same letter. The big brown bear bore down on the boy
- Mention people's names
- Stir people's emotions – people act on what they feel
- Use word pictures
  - Adjectives that make nouns live – the chubby, wide-eyed teenager
  - Multi-sensory phraseology – the hairy, black, eight-legged spider crawled stealthily up my naked leg
  - Personification – 'My heart has a mind of its own'
  - Metaphors/analogies – 'My horse was so slow it was like he was running through thick treacle'
  - Compare the strange with the familiar – 'In an aircraft the engines are like the heart and the instruments are like the brain'
  - Quotations – 'I quote others in order to make myself better understood'
  - Imagery – 'She was like a tightrope walker, balancing her work on one shoulder, her family on her other shoulder and the rest of her life on her head'
  - Suspense – A fairly long pause before coming out with a punch line or important point – always used in the presentation of awards such as the Oscars
  - Anecdotes and stories – The best way to make points, especially humorous ones
- Very seldom, if ever, use a swear word
- Testimonials add credibility – That's why sportspeople are paid so much
- Statistics – Also adds credibility
- Exhibits (where necessary and appropriate)
- Limited use of the word 'I'
- Don't generalise

> End with something that may:
> - Have a twist
> - Leave people with something to physically do
> - Leave people with goose bumps
> - Leave an impact on people
> - Leave people feeling good about themselves (or someone else). Usually you always want people to feel good about themselves
> Avoid:
> - Dull laundry lists (like all these bullet points!!!)
> - Clichés
> - Old jokes
> Style
> - Develop your own style, but whatever it is, the speech must flow freely and easily, with one thought leading naturally into the next
> Intermittent reinforcement
> - At appropriate intervals remind the audience of your purpose. To this end a catchphrase may be very appropriate and can be repeated a number of times during the speech
>   - An excellent example of this is the election campaign of Barack Obama. He would deliver a few lines ending with a rhetorical question and answer it himself: 'Yes we can.' This happened a number of times during his speeches until it became his election slogan. The crowds would answer his rhetorical questions in unison, 'Yes we can!' Extremely simple wording yet memorable and powerful.

Having written the speech, ask yourself whether every sentence, in fact every word, fulfils your objective of directing the audience what to think, feel and do after the speech? If not, eliminate superfluous words and sentences and keep the message clear and simple. If necessary have a number of drafts until you are satisfied.

Delivery

The entire point of the delivery is to be in command of the audience so that they remain focused and interested in what you are saying. They must be hanging on to every word and hungry to hear the next word, delivered with confidence and authority

- ➢ Posture
    - Before you start pause for a few seconds, remaining silent until the audience is silent
    - Stand tall, but relaxed
    - Centre yourself
    - Stand square – head, shoulders, feet, torso
    - Hands by your side if notes are on a lectern
    - Hold notes high
    - Stay square and upright throughout the speech
    - Avoid:
        - ○ Shifting from side to side
        - ○ Standing on one side
        - ○ Hands clasped in front or behind
        - ○ Rocking back and forth
        - ○ Nervous movements
- ➢ Voice projection
    - Hold head high
    - Don't talk down
    - Enunciate your words
- ➢ Voice level
    - Speak normally
        - ○ Not too loud
        - ○ Not too soft (unless to **emphasise** a point or by way of illustration)
        - ○ Voice inflection very good
        - ○ Not a monotone
        - ○ Change pace, inflection, modulation, but not too often

- ○ Accents and impersonating people's accents can be funny, provided they are not humiliating
- ➤ Pace and rhythm
  - Speak at a comfortable, normal pace unless you want to make a point by slowing down or accelerating
- ➤ Pause
  - Before and after making a point
  - Before a punch line
  - After a thought when you want people to digest what you've said
  - Before or after a telling gesture
  - Pauses are the soul of the speech and can be as important as the words themselves – imagine a speech where the speaker rushes through the entire speech without a pause
  - Timing of the pauses is also important – too short and you haven't made the point, too long and the audience may be lost
- ➤ Gestures – can be very powerful (a picture is worth 1,000 words)
  - Emphasis
  - Illustration
  - Humour
  - Every gesture, like every word, must be directed towards the purpose of the speech
  - One or two gestures in themselves can live longer in people's memories than words (good or bad – think of Chamberlain waving the white paper)
- ➤ Props
  - The right prop can be extremely effective because people can see it and it may be the one thing that they remember. If you can find the one image that encapsulates your entire message with a prop, then you will have scored a home run
  - For instance, if you were giving a speech on the horrors of smoking and you produced an actual diseased lung, black and collapsed, you probably wouldn't have to say much more
  - Hopefully you won't be giving such depressing speeches, but you get the idea

- ➢ Eye contact, sweep
  - Essential to make eye contact and hold for a couple of seconds with audience around the room
- ➢ Microphone – have radio mike or podium if possible
  - Speak directly into the microphone at the same distance at all times
- ➢ Use of notes
  - Depending on your level of confidence you can have either:
    - ○ The full written out speech in front of you
    - ○ Notes or cards (detailed or less detailed)
    - ○ Either way, unless you are extremely accomplished it is usually not a good idea to deliver the speech by heart without any safety net, as impressive as it looks to speak totally without notes.
    - ○ **In all cases you still need to know the speech extremely well and have practised it a few times**
  - If you use only notes, hold them at chest level so that you only need to glance at them occasionally, thus maintaining eye contact with the audience
  - The same goes for a speech written out in full
  - It is best to have a lectern which will leave your hands and arms free for gestures
  - If you have the speech written out in full you should know it very well so that you know what's coming and you only have to occasionally glance down at the speech, thus maintaining eye contact with the audience
  - You must not read key words and phrases which are humorous or making a strong point. These must be known by heart and delivered looking at the audience
  - If possible, do not just read the speech. It could lose its impact
- ➢ Appearance
  - Dress appropriately. If a tie and jacket is expected, don't turn up in jeans and trainers. If the occasion is very casual, smart dress may be inappropriate. But never look sloppy, even at casual

functions. 'If there are 12 *clowns* in a ring, you can jump in the middle and start *reciting Shakespeare*, but to the audience, you'll just be the thirteenth *clown*'

- ➢ Be a student of public speaking. Observe speakers, good and bad, for content and delivery
  - What do they do or say that:
    - The audience likes?
    - The audience doesn't like? **(You can learn a great deal from a bad speech knowing what not to do)**
    - You find interesting, amusing?
    - Irritates you?
    - Works/Doesn't work
    - Uses words, quotations, imagery etc. well
  - How do they use notes?
  - What is their posture like?
  - Do they maintain eye contact?
  - Do they stand square?

Preparation Before Making the Speech – Vital to Ensure Confidence

- ➢ Practice with friends/family. (You may consider joining Toastmasters or the Association of Speakers' Clubs, if there is a chapter in your region)
- ➢ You can practice in a mirror if you are comfortable with that
- ➢ Make sure speech is within time frame
- ➢ Know your final speech very well (not necessary to know by heart), so don't have to read off pat
- ➢ **Visualisation**
  - I'm confident and authoritative when I deliver this speech on …
  - I'm relaxed and inspiring when I speak at the … on … (you can make up your own visualisations)

- o **Repeating these visualisations to yourself on many occasions before the speech is extremely important.** They can be said before going to sleep and early on waking up.

The greatest confidence builder is that you believe you have an excellent speech that you know well. The speech is clear in its message and you know exactly what you want the audience to do.

It's not about you – it's about what you are supposed to be speaking about – people's interests or needs or someone else.

Be Yourself

- ➤ You are unique and you have been invited to speak because of who you are. Don't try to be anybody else.

Respect your audience.

Authority does not mean arrogance. It means being in control of the situation. Confidence does not mean cockiness. It is a quiet belief in yourself. It does not exclude humility and the knowledge that you are not perfect or always right. You need genuine confidence to succeed in anything you do. You also need to take risks to succeed.

About the Author

Arnie Witkin was born in Johannesburg in 1944. After qualifying as a chartered accountant he went to London in 1966. From a closeted and insular upbringing he was thrown into the deep end of the swimming pool of life. The only person he knew was his 17-year-old cousin. Lonely, afraid and with enough money to last him two months the adventure that seemed so exciting as he was leaving Durban harbour three weeks earlier was suddenly daunting. He had to find accommodation, get a job and organise a social life. He made copious notes on his strategies for coping and making plans. He succeeded in all aspects, despite his initial immaturity and reticence. He knows what young adults are going through.   In 1968 he returned to South Africa and went into the investment business. He was one of the most successful fund managers in the late 1970s and early 1980s. In 1982 he started the first formalised private equity companies in the country along US lines. He informally was known as the 'Father of private equity' in the country.

Having been involved in three highly successful private equity companies, in 2001 he was diagnosed with advanced thyroid cancer which had spread to his greater laryngeal nerve. It had to be severed resulting in him being unable to speak other than in a high pitched whisper until corrected by surgery three years later. Due to his compromised health he retired from active business in 2004. In 2009 the cancer became active again and spread to his lungs. At around the same time he was diagnosed with prostate cancer and had to have a prostatectomy.

He went onto a chemotherapy drug for 19 months which seemed to hold the cancer in check until June 2019. He went back on the drug, which has stabilised the condition.

Since 2004 he has been an executive coach and mentor, speech writer and public speaking coach. He has spoken at major investment conferences and at an international conference on private equity. He has been a confidant to chief executives at the highest level of business as well as a cabinet minister. He has mentored aspiring and more established entrepreneurs. Children and adult grandchildren of his friends consult him with their issues, knowing that they will be heard with the utmost respect and not preached to. He is non-judgemental and people of all ages, religion, gender and colour are comfortable with him. His focus is on getting people to take responsibility for themselves, to make plans and to take action.

He has been married for 47 years and has two children and six grandchildren. He has at times been in fairly dire financial straits and has been very successful. He has had to overcome major health, career and financial setbacks at every stage of life. He has a deep understanding of the human condition at all ages.

He would like to share his stories and insights with his grandchildren and all grandchildren everywhere, as well as with their parents and grandparents.

What people are saying about *It's Not A Big Thing In Life* ...

'There are so many aha moments in this invaluable guide: what you thought you knew and didn't; what you tried to tell your kids and couldn't; what priorities you'd sorted and hadn't. Invaluable for young (the "target audience") and old (unexpected beneficiaries) *It's Not A Big Thing In Life* presents life lessons learned with humour, honesty and the courage of the personal.'

Reina Teeger

'What I found so appealing about the book is that it was your gift to your GROWN-UP grandchildren who TIME will prevent from ever "contemplating the universe" with you. Shared by a concerned, loving, witty grandpa, these carefully considered life skills, emerging from the struggles and triumphs of your own universe, will speak wisely, gently and humorously as your grandkids read your storied revelations. Already some grownups, who aren't your grandchildren, have thanked you for some significant life decisions. *It's Not A Big Thing In Life* is absorbing and fun to read. It's not your regular 'how to' book.'

Lynnette Baskind

'Ever since I can remember, my grandpa has been a constant source of insight, wisdom and advice. When I was a very small child in London, he and I would sit in these big chairs and "contemplate the universe". He taught me at a very young age some of the most important things I know today. Amongst many other things, I learned about the value of family and loved ones, to listen and keep an open mind to others' thoughts, to strive for happiness and to differentiate between the really big things from those that aren't big things in life. I will always hold these values close, thank you Grandpa.'

Sarah Witkin, oldest grandchild

What people are saying about *It's Not A Big Thing In Life* ...

'This book is one that I believe all beings, young or old, parent or child and grandparent or grandchild, should take the time to read. The stories are expressed in a manner that is both authentic and raw. Real experiences shared by a real person whose wisdom truly resonates. There is a nugget on every page. Reading *It's Not A Big Thing In Life* has allowed me to be kinder to myself and to the world around me. I now feel empowered to take on matters of the heart and the mind with a fresh perspective and powerful perceptions.'

Talya Matuson

'The book is an engaging journey that has related to me in more ways than I care to mention, I sense we had an extremely similar childhood/ adolescent journey. The book has made me smile, laugh, wince and despair, often taking me back to my journey transitioning from a boy to man. I love that there are stories from your own personal experiences that at times are extremely revealing. This helps me as the reader to relate as someone who has experienced so many of them for myself and it brings a sense of comfortability and warmth to me.'

Ian Clark

'Thank you for entertaining me over the past few days with your book for your grandchildren, and other people's. It is beautifully written and interesting – a concise distillation of your life's learning. Adjectives that come to mind are witty, wise, considerate, caring, kind, modest, and strong. You practice what you preach, in the kindest, most self-deprecating manner. I would love for my children, grandchildren and especially my husband to read it.'

Estelle Doctor

'I would very much recommend this book to my children and grandchildren. They would benefit enormously. Even at this advanced age, I learned a lot of valuable life lessons.'

Bess Teeger